Global Korea

South Korea's Contributions to International Security

COUNCIL *on*
FOREIGN
RELATIONS

Scott Bruce, John Hemmings,
Balbina Hwang, Terence Roehrig,
and Scott A. Snyder

Global Korea
South Korea's Contributions
to International Security

Contents

Foreword

Scott A. Snyder

The Korean peninsula often comes to mind as a global security flash point. The most recent reminders include North Korea's April 2012 failed test of a multistage rocket and the November 2010 North Korean shelling of South Korea's Yeonpyeong Island. Given the seriousness of the ongoing standoff on the Korean peninsula, South Korea's emergence as an active contributor to international security addressing challenges far from the Korean peninsula is a striking new development, marking South Korea's emergence as a producer rather than a consumer of global security resources.

This short volume outlines South Korea's progress and accomplishments toward enhancing its role and reputation as a contributor to international security. In the chapters that follow my introduction assessing the significance, sustainability, and challenges facing South Korea's global security roles, Balbina Hwang describes South Korea's plans and development of experience in international peacekeeping, including an analysis of South Korea's peacekeeping capabilities and South Korean public views of South Korea's role and capabilities. Terence Roehrig discusses South Korean contributions to antipiracy operations in the Gulf of Aden, including a detailed description of the commitments and capabilities surrounding a successful South Korean commando operation to recover the *Samho Jewelry* in January 2011. John Hemmings analyzes the challenges and valuable lessons learned from South Korea's establishment of a Provincial Reconstruction Team in Afghanistan, including the civilian-military coordination challenges that accompanied that operation. Finally, Scott Bruce describes South Korea's commitments and capabilities to implement counterproliferation operations, which remain of particular relevance given concerns about North Korea's ability and willingness to sell nuclear materials to the highest bidder.

The CFR program on U.S.-Korea policy would like to acknowledge the Korea Foundation and the Smith Richardson Foundation for their support of the project, and to thank the East Asia Institute for hosting a valuable workshop held in December 2011 in Seoul, at which the chapter authors benefited from the critical review of their initial drafts by Korean experts. Additional programmatic support from Korea International Trade Association and Hyundai Motors America has enabled the production and distribution of this volume. Senior Vice President and Director of Studies James M. Lindsay and Director for Editorial Strategy Anya Schmemann provided valuable comments that strengthened the final product. CFR Publications staff Patricia Dorff and Lia Norton ably edited and managed the production of the publication. Finally, I would like to thank my research associate Paul Choi for managing the project and publication process.

Overview

Scott A. Snyder

South Korea has gradually expanded its contributions to international security in recent years through increased participation in peacekeeping, antipiracy, postconflict stabilization, counterproliferation, and other activities designed to safeguard global stability. These contributions build on those from the late 1990s and early 2000s, including the dispatch of peacekeepers as part of United Nations (UN) stabilization operations in East Timor and Cyprus in the late 1990s and of a special unit to contribute to the stabilization of Iraq beginning in 2003. Prior to these operations, the last major Korean military operations off the Korean peninsula involved South Korean contributions of military forces to the conflict in Vietnam in the late 1960s and early 1970s.

Within the past five years, the scale and level of South Korean contributions to international security operations have expanded noticeably in line with the emphasis on South Korean president Lee Myung-bak's references to a "global Korea." Under this initiative, South Korea has sought to raise its global profile and contributions to the international community not only by hosting meetings such as the Group of Twenty (G20), but also by more actively participating in both development and security around the world. South Korea's increased profile as a contributor to international security is striking because it has traditionally, since the Korean War in the 1950s, been considered a consumer rather than a producer of security resources. Despite the ongoing threat posed by North Korea, however, South Korea is becoming a producer of security resources off the Korean peninsula in response to international needs, contributing to the provision of public goods as a responsible participant in and beneficiary of the world trading system. South Korea's economic growth and modernization has enabled it to build the capacity, interest, and resources necessary to make contributions to global security.

By manpower, South Korea is the sixth-largest military in the world. According to the Stockholm International Peace Research Institute,

South Korea had the twelfth-largest military expenditures in 2010, just ahead of established middle powers such as Australia and Canada, representing an expansion of capacity that has enabled its contributions to international security beyond the peninsula.[1] As long as the situation on the peninsula remains stable, the South Korean government has the appropriate capacities to meet the specific international need, and the government is able to maintain public support for contributions to stabilization and peacekeeping operations, South Korea is well positioned to make important niche contributions to international stability.

Indeed, South Korea's increased contributions to global security are one of three national defense priorities, alongside ongoing efforts to ensure security on the Korean peninsula. South Korea's 2010 defense white paper identifies "contributing to regional stability and world peace" as one of three national defense objectives, along with "defending the nation from external military threats and invasion" and "upholding the principle of peaceful unification." To support these activities, the Republic of Korea (ROK) has established a three-thousand-person standing unit dedicated to overseas deployments; passed legislation authorizing the deployment of up to one thousand ROK personnel to UN peacekeeping operations (PKO) before requiring an authorization request from the ROK National Assembly; and established a PKO center dedicated to the training of military personnel to be dispatched for overseas assignments.[2] This is a significant new development that, with South Korean public support and in the absence of major instability or tension on the Korean peninsula, shows South Korea's willingness to contribute to international security for the long haul.

As a top-twenty global economy that depends on trade for its economic growth, South Korea has an interest in contributing to global stability to protect a primary source of the country's hard-won prosperity. Envisioning a more active South Korean role on the international stage based on its own economic modernization and political development, South Korean president Lee Myung-bak pledged in his inaugural address to "carry out global diplomacy under which we actively cooperate with the international community. Respecting the universal principles of democracy and market economics, we will take part in the global movement for peace and development."[3] Since his inauguration in 2008, Lee has fulfilled his pledge by contributing South Korea's military and technological capabilities to stabilization and peacekeeping missions in Haiti, Lebanon, the Gulf of Aden, and Afghanistan. South

Korea's multifaceted efforts to establish itself as a provider rather than merely a consumer of security go hand in hand with its transformation from recipient to provider of international development assistance, making available additional resources to preserve stability at a time when traditional aid and security providers in the United States and Europe are facing increased fiscal constraints.

EVOLUTION OF SOUTH KOREA'S DEBATE OVER ITS CONTRIBUTIONS TO INTERNATIONAL SECURITY

South Korean debates over the country's international security role have historically been framed primarily in the context of the U.S.-ROK security alliance, either as a down payment on the extension of a U.S. security presence on the Korean peninsula or as an "involuntary" contribution resulting from South Korea's dependency on the United States to meet South Korean security needs. South Koreans have historically worried that resources expended off the peninsula might come at the expense of South Korea's ability to meet the ostensibly overwhelming threat posed by North Korea. For U.S. security planners, an occasional source of conflict with South Korea has been the latter's seemingly narrow vision of security, which has traditionally been confined to the peninsula at the expense of a broader regional and global view. Past South Korean thinking about contributions was inevitably tied to the question of how to strengthen either American assurances or tangible commitments to the security of the Korean peninsula. South Korea's new view of its role reflects a dramatic change in this self-assessment, which for the first time delinks South Korea's role in and contributions to international security from the U.S.-ROK alliance.

The classic example of the old thinking about the relationship between South Korean overseas deployments and the U.S.-ROK alliance was former South Korean president Park Chung-hee's decision to provide South Korean troops in support of American war aims in Vietnam. At that time, the United States was deeply entangled in conflict in Indochina that threatened to distract from its security obligations in South Korea. Moreover, a belligerent and opportunistic North Korean leadership sought to take advantage of the U.S. preoccupation with the war in Indochina, for instance through the 1968 capture of the

USS *Pueblo* in waters near North Korea. Worried that U.S. commitment to South Korea might waver in the face of heavy burdens in Vietnam, Park sent South Korean infantry troops to fight in Vietnam, where they built a reputation as a fearsome fighting force. Park's reasoning for sending the troops was tied to South Korea's security dependency on the United States and Park's worry that American distraction might lead to renewed North Korean adventurism at the expense of South Korea. Thus, South Korea weighed its decision on whether to contribute troops to Vietnam purely within the context of concerns about U.S. abandonment of South Korea's security needs vis-à-vis North Korea.

A more recent manifestation of tensions between South Korea's prioritization of its security needs against U.S. demands for out-of-area contributions came in 2003 and 2004 at a time of relative tension in the U.S.-ROK alliance. At that time, the United States requested that friends and allies, including South Korea, contribute military forces to help stabilize the security situation in Iraq following the Persian Gulf War. This request for assistance came to the Roh Moo-hyun administration in 2003, along with informal notice that the operational demands of the Iraq War would also require the United States to relocate a brigade of the Second Infantry Division based in Seoul to Iraq. This onward assignment of 3,600 American troops was disturbing to Seoul, coming as it did in the midst of political differences between Washington and Seoul over how to coordinate policy toward North Korea.

The Roh Moo-hyun administration responded to Washington's request by attempting to negotiate a more flexible U.S. policy toward North Korea as a quid pro quo for South Korean troops in Iraq, a request that American officials brusquely deflected as unseemly and contrary to the spirit of the long-standing alliance relationship. On the other hand, progressive South Korean officials clearly felt entrapped by the alliance: they could not easily avoid a U.S. request for assistance at the same time that South Korea disagreed with and felt endangered by the Bush administration's hard-line policies toward North Korea.

The issue of a South Korean troop contribution to Iraq was defined by the Roh administration wholly as a U.S.-ROK alliance matter, for which South Korea sought due recognition from the United States on the basis of its ultimately contributing the third-largest contingent of military forces to Iraq. But Seoul's decision to define the U.S. request for military assistance primarily as an alliance contribution served to politicize the U.S.-ROK alliance unnecessarily. It also revealed South

Korean public concerns about the risk of involvement in international entanglements, as exemplified by weak initial public support for South Korea's troop dispatch to Iraq. The dispatch was finally approved at the National Assembly on a rare bipartisan vote in which an independent group of ruling party members combined with the conservative opposition. Months later, the South Korean contribution in Irbil proved to be a success on the ground, but South Korean officials rankled over the Bush administration's failure to give sufficient acknowledgment to the government of South Korea for its contributions. Once again, South Korean deliberations over whether to contribute to stabilization in Iraq were conducted exclusively in the context of how to manage the alliance with the United States and how to manage policy differences over North Korea, rather than with regard to South Korea's stake in promoting international stability.

A "GLOBAL KOREA" AND SOUTH KOREA'S INTERESTS IN GLOBAL SECURITY

The Lee Myung-bak administration, however, has taken a different approach to South Korean contributions to international security with the aim of establishing what it calls a "global Korea." After an initial period of caution and concern about the need to ensure public support for a larger South Korean role in global security at the beginning of his administration, President Lee was able to raise South Korea's profile, capabilities, and willingness to contribute to international security in tandem with broader efforts to raise the country's profile as a leader on the world stage. To this end, South Korea has stepped up its efforts to show leadership in multilateral global forums by hosting the G20 in Seoul in November 2010, the Organization for Economic Cooperation and Development (OECD) Development Assistance Committee's (DAC) High-Level Forum in Busan in November 2011, and the nuclear security summit in March 2012.

President Lee stated in his 2011 New Year's speech that "a crucial goal of this administration has been to build a Global Korea," in which he identified contributions to international development, green growth, and economic growth through free trade agreements as components of the strategy. In a subsequent speech at a conference commemorating the fourth anniversary of his inauguration, Lee stated that "the Global

Korea initiative puts emphasis on helping countries in need, while contributing proactively to the peace and prosperity of all peoples."

President Lee has provided a compelling rationale for South Korea to make contributions to less fortunate countries, both as part of South Korea's global responsibilities and as a way of acknowledging and reciprocating international assistance that made vital contributions to South Korea's survival and rapid development. Thus, South Korea's roles in and contributions to international security are no longer being defined by its government as U.S.-ROK alliance issues, but as issues of South Korea's responsibilities and interests in promoting global stability as a leading member of the international community.

As a result, South Korea is no longer seeking credit for its contributions in the eyes of the United States or as a contribution to the U.S.-ROK alliance; instead, it is contributing to international security based on its capabilities and interests. This shift is evidence of a maturation of South Korea's conception of its role in the world that helps establish the country as a leader that does not pursue its foreign policy interests solely through the lens of the U.S.-ROK security alliance. South Korea deserves both acknowledgment and credit for its sense of international responsibility and for its efforts to establish itself as a country capable of making tangible contributions and providing leadership within the world community.

Today, South Korea has developed substantial experience in a variety of peacekeeping operations since it first contributed an engineering battalion to Somalia in 1993. South Korea currently contributes 637 personnel to nine UN peacekeeping operations, making it the thirty-third-largest contributor of personnel to UN-led peacekeeping operations. It is also the tenth-largest contributor of funds to the 2011–2012 UN peacekeeping budget, with a share representing 2.7 percent of the annual budget. A solid contributor to Combined Task Force (CTF)-151, South Korea has the capacity to keep two destroyers operational as part of the mission on an ongoing basis. In addition, it is contributing a Provincial Reconstruction Team (PRT) of 336 personnel in Afghanistan along with $93.416 million in assistance in 2010 via the overseas Korea International Cooperation Agency (KOICA).[4] Although South Korea was relatively late to join the Proliferation Security Initiative (PSI)—it did so only two days after North Korea's May 2009 nuclear test—it has become an active participant in the group and has heeded the call to strengthen both its export control over dangerous or prohibited items and its cooperation with others in this regard.

KOREA'S CONTRIBUTIONS

The June 2009 U.S.-ROK Joint Vision Statement formally defines the application of the U.S.-ROK bilateral alliance as extending beyond the Korean peninsula to meet regional and global challenges.[5] The joint vision statement proposes an expanded role for the U.S.-ROK alliance in contributing to international security. It is underpinned by both an increase in South Korean capabilities and a South Korean willingness to step forward and make such capabilities available as a public good for use within the international community. The statement also anticipates that South Korea will make contributions to security commensurate with the benefits it derives from a stable global system.

The obligation to support the United States because of the U.S.-ROK alliance is no longer the dominant South Korean interest in contributing to international security. However, the alliance can continue to provide a solid platform for South Korean regional and global missions, both by assisting South Korean efforts to extend its capabilities in international stabilization and peacekeeping efforts and by making South Korea's contributions more effective in concert with the efforts of other actors.

South Korea's enhanced capability and willingness to contribute to international security improve its value as a partner to the United States, which in turn adds value to the U.S.-ROK alliance. As long as the alliance has available resources and is able to muster public support in both countries, the United States should seek a close partnership with South Korea to strengthen South Korean contributions in various international coalitions. In some cases, prior relationships developed through alliance-based cooperation on the peninsula might facilitate new working relationships in an entirely different operating environment, for instance, as partners in establishing stability and promoting development in Afghanistan. In other cases, cooperation between like-minded countries, such as the United States and ROK, will be a valuable asset that can be used to build political support for international stabilization operations.

The U.S.-ROK alliance may also benefit from practical forms of cooperation and interoperability that are being honed through practical experience that cannot be replicated by scenario-based exercises alone. Both countries face the need to more prudently allocate defense budgets, and the experience of working together may also produce opportunities to cooperate in ways that do not unduly limit loss of specific capabilities. Moreover, as the United States moves to emphasize greater interaction and lateral networking of capabilities among Asian bilateral alliances, South Korea's experience working in a multinational environment will provide a valuable base of experience from which to operate.

An enhanced South Korean role in international security will provide residual benefits for the development of South Korean experience and capabilities, particularly in light of the possibility that prolonged instability in North Korea would likely require South Korea to accomplish some tasks that are part of stabilization or peacekeeping operations in other countries. For this reason, South Korea's exposure to many types of fragile or failed-state situations and direct involvement in postconflict stabilization operations may prove to be invaluable practical experience that can be applied to the management of potential future instability in North Korea.

POTENTIAL OBSTACLES TO CONTINUED CONTRIBUTIONS

Although the catchphrase *global Korea* seems appropriate to provide a framework for analyzing South Korea's stepped-up contributions to international security, it is not clear to what extent South Korea's emerging contributions are sustainable. Scenarios that could cause South Korea to reduce its international activities include a crisis in North Korea, a withdrawal of domestic public support in South Korea for stabilization operations, or economic and demographic constraints that could limit South Korea's capacity to make future contributions to international security.

The potential instability in North Korea is the most significant threat to sustaining South Korean contributions to international security. For instance, the March 2010 sinking of the *Cheonan* exposed a need for South Korea's navy to invest in antisubmarine warfare capabilities; such a significant investment arguably could have distracted from recent South Korean investments in expeditionary naval capabilities to carry out operations far from the Korean peninsula. In the end, South Korea invested in both capabilities. This example suggests that indeed South Korea is capable of providing contributions to both international stability and security on the Korean peninsula. But there is always the possibility that a significant flare-up of inter-Korean tensions or destabilization of North Korea will cause a shift in resources back to the Korean peninsula, and a prolonged focus on the task of restoring Korean peninsular and East Asian regional stability. In fact, this circumstance could well exceed South Korean resources and turn the country once again into a consumer of international security resources, requiring significant support from the United States and the world community as well. Although the level of resources in South Korea, Japan, and even China that might be used to stabilize North Korea is considerable, political and donor coordination challenges would require substantial international attention and resources.

Second, the sustainability of South Korea's political commitment to maintain active contributions to international security will be tested by the eventual political transition to a new administration in South Korea in February 2013 that may or may not be as committed to using South Korean resources for global security. However, given the level of South Korean dependency on the world trading system, it is hard to envision a dramatic shift in South Korean priorities that would curtail South Korean participation in international stability operations. Another possibility is if there were an uptick in South Korean casualties from such operations. Certainly, such an occurrence would catalyze an active political debate in South Korea over the nature and purpose of its international involvement. But it is unlikely that South Korea will abandon the perceived prestige benefits that accrue to its reputation as an active and positive leader in the world community, including its contributions to international security.

Third, South Korea will face demographic and budget constraints in the midterm that could eventually pressure it to reduce its commitments to international security. For instance, if South Korea shifts from mandatory conscription to a volunteer army, the size of the military force would likely shrink. In addition, the country's birth rate is well below replacement rates, meaning that available manpower to serve in South Korea's military will gradually shrink from current levels. Such constraints, however, are unlikely in the next five to ten years. In addition, those constraints may be less important if inter-Korean tensions are reduced, in which case there could actually be considerable room for South Korea to become an even greater contributor in the international security field.

Given the strong commitment of South Korea's leadership, the public's acceptance of South Korea's expanded role and its appreciation for the prestige such a role confers, and the country's strong and growing economy, it is likely that South Korea will continue to play a constructive role beyond its own borders. Each of the potential obstacles outlined has the capacity to derail future South Korean contributions to international security. However, South Korean desires to play a greater role on the world stage appear to be strong enough that despite these obstacles, the country will continue to make modest contributions to international security.

SUSTAINING SOUTH KOREA'S GROWING ROLE: RECOMMENDATIONS

An outward-oriented South Korea capable of contributing positively to the international community generates goodwill and recognition of South Korea's international contributions and provides benefits to the world and to the United States, given the convergence of U.S. and South Korean interests in strengthening a liberal, economically open global system. The U.S.-ROK alliance is a ready-made platform to support South Korean contributions to international stability, but recognizes that South Korean contributions to global peace and security should be based on South Korean national interest and not on alliance considerations. The following recommendations would strengthen and extend South Korea's contributions to international security.

Combine South Korea's instruments of hard and soft power to enhance the effectiveness of its international security contributions. South Korea's emerging military capabilities, along with its efforts to expand its budget for international aid by capitalizing on its successful experience with development, provide an opportunity to combine the two to underscore its growing stature and responsibility in the world community. South Korea should continue to use its military capabilities and development experience in combination to strengthen its profile as a constructive actor on the global stage.

Invest in stabilization missions abroad so that the lessons of international experience are available to be applied at home. South Korea's involvement in postconflict stabilization missions abroad provides it the benefit of learning how to merge security and development provisions in the absence of an effective government in North Korea. South Korean participation in postconflict stabilization elsewhere provides valuable experience in the event that instability in North Korea results in state failure and the necessity to restore order in the northern part of the Korean peninsula.

Grasp the opportunity to show leadership on nuclear nonproliferation commensurate with South Korea's growing interest in the export of nuclear plants. South Korea's participation in activities such as PSI and its leadership in strengthening export controls are important contributions to the prevention of proliferation. South Korea should seek to augment its human and financial contributions to strengthen the International Atomic Energy Agency (IAEA) and to build greater regional awareness of the need to uphold international nonproliferation norms through the East Asian Summit (EAS), especially given its emergence as a nuclear energy exporter.

Apply South Korea's leadership role in international security to the Asian regional context. South Korea's establishment of a three-thousand-person force dedicated to contributing to international stabilization missions provides South Korea with a capability to contribute to stability anywhere in the world. Thus far, South Korean peacekeeping forces have responded primarily to crises outside Asia. But this capability might also serve as a catalyst to develop and strengthen regional capabilities and structures for cooperation within Asia, especially in response to complex humanitarian emergencies. South Korea may also be in a position to provide both capacity and leadership in building effective regional cooperation within Asia, where effective tools for responding to crisis and managing instability have been slow to develop. It could make a valuable contribution to a strengthened regional crisis response capability by contributing resources to respond to complex humanitarian emergencies and other forms of instability in the region.

In sum, South Korea stands to strengthen its local, regional, and global position and to contribute in a helpful and constructive way to international security if it applies its development experience abroad, takes lessons from stabilization missions to apply to potential instability on the Korean peninsula, promotes the peaceful and lawful use of nuclear power, and participates in operations in Asia. These steps will consolidate South Korea's contributions to international security and provide a return on its investment by promoting the stability necessary for it to rely on the world trading system for its development.

If South Korea can sustain this broadened role, it will be a positive development both for South Korea's role in the world and for U.S.-ROK alliance cooperation, especially because it will allow the United States and South Korea to pursue shared interests across a broader spectrum of activities, with greater potential effect on prospects for maintaining regional and global stability. But it remains to be seen whether South Korea can maintain and expand these commitments, whether its economy will continue to allow it to spend the significant resources required, and whether its leadership and public will remain committed to the vision of a global Korea. For now, if South Korea can face the obstacles outlined and pursue the recommendations suggested here, its global role seems likely to grow and mature.

Korea and PKO:
Is Korea Contributing to Global Peace?

Balbina Hwang

South Korea is well recognized for having transformed itself within the span of one generation from an impoverished, war-torn society into a modern, developed, and democratic nation. This success has propelled the Republic of Korea (ROK) for the first time in Korea's long history onto the global stage with the capability to have a positive influence far beyond the peninsula.

GLOBAL KOREA

President Lee Myung-bak's international leadership profile has become synonymous with his vision of a global Korea. Yet the idea of a global strategy for South Korea is decades old, having initially been articulated and implemented as a national strategy of globalization, or *segyehwa*, by the Kim Young-sam administration in 1993. Indeed, as Samuel Kim observes, no other state in the post–Cold War era cast its lot with globalization quite as publicly as South Korea did in the 1990s.[1] The country's policy of globalization was meant to describe its unique way of promoting political, economic, social, and cultural enhancement to reach the level of most advanced nations in the world. Han Sung-joo, South Korea's foreign minister at the time, articulated *segyehwa* as the main component of South Korea's new diplomacy (*sin oegyo*) in May 1993, characterizing the latter as being composed of five basic themes relevant for South Korean foreign policy outlook: globalism, diversification, multidimensionalism, regional cooperation, and future orientation. Han's vision thus embraced a more traditional definition of globalization, one in which South Korea would be more active in the international arena:

With the advent of the era of globalism, [South] Korea's diplomacy needs to pay more attention to such universal values as freedom, justice, peace and welfare. We will take an active part in international efforts to tackle global issues such as international peace and security, disarmament and arms control, eradication of poverty, protection of environment, and efficient utilization of natural resources. Through such engagement, we will play our due part in making a more just, safe, and prosperous world.[2]

Notably, however, differences among the dynamics that underlie the formulation, rationalization, and implementation of these strategies are profound. First, although *segyehwa* in 1993 may have articulated visionary principles about expanding South Korea's role in the international arena, in reality it was a singularly myopic view of raising South Korean domestic standards and status. Sweeping changes in the global economy at the time, including loosening international financial capital controls along with heightened protectionist trade measures in developed economies, meant increased economic pressures on the highly export-dependent South Korean economy. In response to these external challenges, President Kim unveiled the *segyehwa* policy, a banner strategy under which he could attempt top-down reforms of the South Korean political economy to meet the rapidly changing conditions of the world economy. And as was typical of many national campaigns, globalization was touted in South Korea as a matter not of choice but of necessity; the national slogan "globalize or perish" in the 1990s replaced the "export or die" mantra of the rapid development era of the 1970s.[3]

Segyehwa ultimately failed to make any significant progress in globalizing the South Korean economy. From 1993 to 1998, the period of Kim's presidency, South Korea's economic performance actually declined noticeably, according to standard indicators, and included a steady drop in globalization rankings.[4] In large part, this is because the vision was and remained merely for the future. South Korea lacked the capabilities, infrastructure, and political capacity to implement in any meaningful manner a truly global role for itself. During the past two decades, however, it has developed the commensurate means to truly support the leadership's articulated vision of a global Korea.

THE ROK'S PEACEKEEPING ACTIVITIES

The cornerstone of South Korea's global Korea strategy is to embrace international responsibilities and actively contribute to resolve global challenges, and one of the most visible and tangible examples has been peacekeeping activities. United Nations (UN) peacekeeping operations (PKOs) first began as an effort by the international community to manage complex crises that posed threats to international peace and security, and have since evolved into one of the UN's main tools to achieve stability in trouble spots around the world. The UN's first operation was in Palestine with the establishment of the UN Truce Supervision Organization (UNTSO) in 1948.[5]

The ROK's participation in peacekeeping operations started more recently, beginning with an engineering battalion dispatched to Somalia in 1993. Since then, the ROK has deployed approximately five thousand personnel to sixteen operations in seven regions; today, South Korea remains active in nine operations, ranking it the thirty-third-largest contributor of personnel to UN-led PKOs (see Figure 1).[6]

The active increase in PKO participation was a direct result of concerted actions taken in recent years by the Ministry of Foreign Affairs and Trade (MOFAT) and the Ministry of National Defense (MND) and

FIGURE 1. CURRENT ROK PKO ACTIVITIES (AS OF OCTOBER 2011)

Location	Operation	Type	Contribution
Haiti	MINUSTAH	troop	243
Lebanon	UNIFIL	troop	369
Abyei, Sudan	UNISFA	troop	1
Western Sahara	MINURSO	expert	2
Liberia	UNMIL	expert	1
Kashmir	UNMOGIP	expert	8
East Timor	UNMIT	police	4
Ivory Coast	UNOCI	expert	2
Southern Sudan	UNMISS	expert	6
		TOTAL	637

Source: United Nations, Peacekeeping Fact Sheet, http://www.un.org/en/peacekeeping/operations.

the National Assembly, under the leadership of the Blue House. The three government bureaucracies conducted intensive review sessions on implementing swift and effective participation in PKOs, resulting in the passage of the Law on Participation in United Nations Peacekeeping Operations on December 29, 2009.[7] This law details a definition for UN PKOs that outlines the principles of mission performance as well as the legal basis for establishing standing forces, parliamentary approval procedures for dispatching forces, extension of operations periods, requirements for activity reports to the National Assembly, and the formation and operation of an interministerial body for policy consultation.

The law also authorizes the ROK government to make provisional agreements with the UN on force scales for dispatch, up to one thousand personnel per dispatch, as well as the location of PKO and duration of service, which all require final approval by the National Assembly.[8] The UN has long called on nations to speed up troop deployments to within thirty to ninety days of a decision to participate in a PKO, and the new law in South Korea will shorten the period for dispatching troops to three to four months from the previous six to seven months.

Another important development that has significantly improved the ROK's capacity to participate more robustly in UN-led PKOs is the creation of standing units for overseas deployment of troops. Initiated in December 2009, these units maintain three thousand total troops composed of three subunits of one thousand members each, dedicated to overseas, reserve, and a separate other function. The overseas subunit is dispatched first on request for PKO, allowing the other reserve subunit to rotate for readiness training for the next deployment. The separate subunit focuses on a wide array of other deployment activities, including engineering, medical, military policy, and naval and air transport to provide support for the deployed troops.[9]

Furthermore, in July 2010, the International Peace Support Force (Onnuri Unit) was created, resulting in an even stronger readiness posture for troop deployment. Until then, the Special Warfare Command had operated a special mission team that had trained and prepared deploying troops, but this unit was dissolved and folded under Onnuri, which further contributes to streamlining the dispatch and deployment of troops for overseas PKOs.[10] Finally, the MND has strengthened the PKO Center, which is in charge of training personnel for deployment. On January 1, 2010, the PKO Center was moved from the Joint Staff College to the National Defense University, and it has plans to increase its research and educational functions as well as staff by 2013 from nineteen to twenty-nine.[11]

In addition to activities explicitly organized under a UN command—which are usually limited to monitoring areas of conflict—the ROK has been a participant in operations coordinated under multinational forces (MNF), which have included direct involvement in the settlement of conflicts and reconstruction efforts. These are technically not peacekeeping operations, but reconstruction and stabilization efforts led by the United States have been considered under the broad umbrella of PKO by both the ROK government and the general South Korean public.[12] The two largest such operations have been conducted in Iraq and Afghanistan. They are the most visible and tangible—and politically sensitive—contributions by the ROK to international coalition efforts and to South Korea's alliance with the United States.[13]

In fact, the ROK has contributed far more to global security and stability operations than it often receives credit for, having deployed more than 325,000 troops in total to twenty-two trouble spots in support of a variety of U.S., UN, and other international missions. For the past several decades, the ROK has been one of the most consistent supporters of U.S.-led security operations, contributing substantial troops to the Vietnam War, the 1991 Gulf War, Iraq, and Afghanistan. And in the peacekeeping realm, South Korean participation has been in areas as diverse as Haiti, Somalia, East Timor, Angola, Western Sahara, Georgia, Kashmir, Cyprus, and Lebanon.

Some of these activities have produced significant results beyond what the absolute contribution may indicate. For example, the South Korean presence in Cyprus was a single position, but the first time that an ROK officer had been in the lead command of a UN Peacekeeping Force, bringing both unprecedented prestige and invaluable experience to the South Korean military leadership.[14] And in Lebanon, although the three hundred and fifty troops dispatched are only a small percentage of the total fifteen-thousand-troop United Nations Interim Force in Lebanon (UNIFIL), the ROK is the only formal treaty ally of the United States in UNIFIL, and thus a major strategic partner vis-à-vis American interests, given that the United States does not have a military presence in Lebanon.[15]

South Korean activities in PKO have included humanitarian and medical assistance; maintenance of public order; election supervision; reconstruction of nations suffering from civil war, genocide, and famine; rebuilding public facilities; building new public facilities; and armistice monitoring, patrol, inspection, and mediation. And while the ROK's ranking in terms of personnel deployment may only be thirty-third, it was the tenth-largest donor to the UN peacekeeping budget (2011–2012), contributing nearly 2.7 percent of the annual cost.[16]

Beyond active deployments, the ROK has expanded international cooperation and training exercises, dispatching a platoon of marines to participate for the first time in a multinational peacekeeping exercise held in Mongolia in August 2009; the ROK had previously participated in this annual Khan Quest exercise, since 2006, but only as an observer, sending working-level officers.[17] The ROK has also participated annually in the Global Peace Operations Initiative (GPOI) Capstone Exercise and engaged in exercises with other participants.[18] And in February 2010, for the first time, the ROK navy and marine corps participated in the six-nation Cobra-Gold Exercise, which entails multination combined exercises and humanitarian relief operations.[19]

South Korea's experience with PKOs has been largely successful and they are considered valuable and worthy activities by ROK officials. However, it is only more recently, with the disaster in Haiti, that their appeal has become generally embraced by the South Korean public and they have begun to receive broader support. In response to the devastating earthquake on January 12, 2010, the UN increased its existing PKO mission in Haiti (MINUSTAH[20]), and the ROK government responded quickly to assist in the recovery and reconstruction efforts by dispatching the Danbi Unit, comprising 240 personnel. Danbi was engaged in critical reconstruction activities such as removing the debris from damaged buildings, restoring roads, drilling wells, dredging waterways, and providing medical and quarantine assistance.[21] This deployment was supplemented by a speedy provision of more than $13 million in aid, by far the largest aid package from East Asia and making South Korea one of the largest contributors of aid to Haiti. Notably, a large amount of the aid was raised through private donations, reflecting a strong outpouring of public sympathy and support for the humanitarian disaster. Given the convergence of public sentiment and swift government action, it is no surprise that South Korean participation in PKOs was given a much-needed positive highlight of their contribution to rebuilding societies.

The South Korean public, however, has been less enthusiastic for lower-profile PKO missions such as those in Lebanon and Sudan, and outright hostile toward the two largest MNF operations in Iraq and Afghanistan. The lesson here is that the South Korean public can readily see the benefits—with minimal risk—of PKO efforts in which activities are focused on immediate humanitarian relief efforts. However, in missions such as Lebanon or Sudan, where the emphasis is more on keeping the peace and maintaining physical cessation of violence, public sentiment may be less inclined to support South Korean participation. Iraq and Afghanistan became bitter political battles held hostage—ironically on both sides of the political spectrum—to the view that the South Korean government's decision to deploy troops was primarily a function of South Korean alliance obligations to the United States rather than of any ROK national interests.

THE RATIONALE FOR PKO PARTICIPATION

Indeed, until recently, the strongest argument in public debates for South Korean participation in PKOs has been that doing so will help maintain and enhance the U.S.-ROK alliance. Embedded in this logic is the implication that the ROK is following U.S. direction rather than perceiving any real independent value from such endeavors. Furthermore, the prevalent view was that achievement of South Korean national interests was secondary to preserving the alliance with the United States; in other words, PKOs are but one utilitarian tool of alliance management. This may indeed have been the driving motivation in the past to justify politically sensitive PKO activities, particularly to a skeptical public.

Recently, however, this attitude has begun to change. Haiti may have been the turning point marking this significant adjustment in public sentiments about PKOs. President Lee Myung-bak's public speeches and statements emphasizing South Korea's international responsibilities have routinely reflected the view that South Korea, as a former recipient of international assistance, should give back to the international community. These concepts have been reinforced by the public leadership roles that South Korea undertook in 2010 hosting the Group of 20 (G20) Leaders and Nuclear Security summits. South Koreans have increasingly begun to openly embrace the notion that it now has a duty to respond to global problems.

Whether South Koreans have truly embraced these profound values and whether these are the guiding principles behind increased public support for PKOs, the reality is that PKO participation serves a wide range of South Korea's national interests. These include contributing to regional and global security by preventing further conflict and enhancing stability, raising the ROK's international profile through tangible contributions that are not only commensurate with its global economic status, but go beyond by demonstrating measurable sacrifice, repaying its debt to the international community—twenty-one countries participated in the U.S.-led UN Command to support the ROK during the Korean War[22]—and enhancing the ROK's security by establishing a reputation as a proactive stabilizing force rather than a belligerent one.

This last rationale has the additional benefit of allowing South Korea to differentiate itself proactively from its neighbors China and Japan. Due to China's steadfast foreign policy principle of "noninterference in domestic affairs" and "respect for national sovereignty," Beijing has always been uneasy in contributing to international missions. Yet China has recently rapidly expanded its participation in UN PKO missions. A closer examination of its contributions, however, reveals that a disproportionately large contingent—nearly 80 percent—of its troops is deployed to PKO missions in the resource-rich region of sub-Saharan Africa, which coincides with Beijing's aggressive strategy to secure resources around the world.[23] Moreover, these UN missions placed Chinese forces in close proximity to other potentially lucrative nations not involved in PKOs, such as Angola, Cameroon, Ghana, and Nigeria, allowing these deployments to serve as vehicles to move military troops into strategically valuable areas. There is also a close linkage between Chinese PKO deployments in Africa and corresponding soaring direct investments in cobalt, copper, iron ore, manganese, and other mineral resources.[24]

In Japan, enduring constitutional constraints, pacifist constituencies, and a paralyzed political leadership make any new movements toward increased PKO contributions unlikely. Currently, Japan has a total of only 258 forces deployed on three UN PKO missions.[25] In addition, the sheer scale of the March 2011 tsunami and nuclear disasters combined with an anemic economy further deflate any likely impetus or enthusiasm for a robust campaign to contribute to UN-led PKO activities, despite Japan's ongoing desire to obtain a permanent seat on the UN Security Council.

Thus, South Korea has a unique opportunity within northeast Asia to present itself as a responsible member of the international community, and the only power from northeast Asia able to demonstrate its stated values-based policies of promoting peace, stability, and prosperity into positive action. Given China's increasingly aggressive maritime stance in the Pacific as well as global resource–hungry strategies, and Japan's inability to fully shed the yoke of its dark imperial history, South Korea can present itself as a neutral beacon for impoverished, conflict-ridden societies, many of which also experienced a bitter history of colonization.

Active participation in PKOs also affords the ROK the opportunity to firmly contrast itself with the Democratic People's Republic of Korea (DPRK) as the North continues to isolate itself in the community of international opinion through its belligerent policies and rhetoric. Establishing a clear differentiation with the DPRK is important not only to delegitimize North Korea's threatening behavior, but also to prevent the North from being accepted as a de facto nuclear state. Finally, current ROK investments in global PKOs increase the likelihood of future reciprocity by the international community in the advent of Korean reunification, which will most likely require tremendous foreign assistance.

Other important rationales for participation in PKOs are more practical, such as gaining valuable training and operational exercise for the ROK military and defense personnel. This not only enhances practical field experience, but also helps prepare for the likelihood that a future North Korean contingency is as likely to involve stabilization efforts as direct combat. Beyond the military benefits, participation in multination operations also provides opportunities for South Korean government officials and bureaucracies to learn how to cooperate with foreign counterparts and build relationships and trust with other countries, and improves civil-military operation capabilities. Last, PKO participation allows the ROK to establish an early positive presence in the peacekeeping area that can provide the basis for later economic development by South Korean businesses.

Finally, PKO participation is an integral part of moving the ROK toward full implementation of its defense reform. Specifically, peacekeeping missions afford opportunities for the ROK military to gain direct experience in one of its most important stated goals: to achieve "an information/knowledge-based qualitative structure" in order to better actualize "the central concept of 'jointness' in future warfare."[26] Arguably, two of the most efficient ways for ROK military personnel to gain such knowledge and experience are to engage in operations with a broad exposure to new technologies and methods—keeping risk levels to a minimum—and to train with international forces (other than American) and in areas off the Korean peninsula.

CONSTRAINTS ON KOREA'S FUTURE PKO

South Korea's rapidly growing appetite for outward global expansion and its impulse to do so across a wide range of issues and venues, combined with its commitment to strengthen and transform its alliance with the United States, offer the possibility for a distinctive U.S.-ROK partnership in the future. Yet Victor Cha observes that "history has shown that Seoul sometimes remains constrained by a version of its own parochialism, which has often stood in the way of elevating the alliance to an international role."[27] Thus, South Korea's singular priority on North Korea ultimately diverted policies, such as *segye-hwa*, which began as lofty visions of expanding South Korea's regional or global presence beyond the peninsula, but faltered as they became eclipsed by policy toward the North.[28] However, taking advantage of a foundation established a decade earlier and changing conditions in the domestic and international environment, the Lee Myung-bak administration's venture to establish a meaningful leadership role for the ROK in the international community has clearly borne fruit. Nevertheless, as President Lee winds down his administration and the ROK faces new leadership in 2013, a number of potential constraints stand in the way of South Korea's continuation down a global path.

The most challenging of these is rooted in South Korea's complex social and political environment—ironically a testament to the remarkable success of U.S. patronage under the alliance—which enabled a vibrant if noisome democratic society to emerge and flourish. Although democratic consolidation in the South Korean political system has reached a certain maturity, leadership institutions remain fragile and are particularly vulnerable to attacks from opposition forces. Complicating matters more is that although the opposition may be highly organized and well represented by political interests, disagreements are deeply rooted to social cleavages. Such conflicts are therefore particularly enduring, often immune to political compromise, and scarcely consensus oriented. It is not surprising, then, that a recent OECD study measuring social conflict around the world ranked the ROK as the fourth worst among twenty-seven member nations.[29]

Although a seemingly puzzling phenomenon, particularly in such a famously homogenous society such as South Korea,[30] social conflict has increased with political democratization because political freedoms were unleashed so suddenly in 1987 on a society that had traditionally been highly regulated by rigid customs and rules and was unaccustomed to a culture that permitted, much less encouraged, personal liberties such as individual expression. Amplifying this dynamic was the unexpectedly equalizing power and rapid proliferation of modern technology—particularly the Internet—that both empowered citizens with anonymous and unfettered license to make their voices heard and allowed for efficient and cheap methods of organizing like-minded groups. Underneath these modern changes on the surface remained a long historical tradition deeply rooted in Confucianism of opposing social or political injustice.[31] Bitterly played out in Korea's recent history during the Japanese occupation and then under decades of authoritarian rule in the ROK, historical opposition figures glorified for their heroism remain fresh in the consciousness of modern South Koreans. In today's current environment, public dissatisfaction with the government is manifested in mass protests and demonstrations, but they often lack unity of purpose and more often than not give off the air of social outings rather than serious political expression.

South Korea's two most recent leaders, former president Roh Moo-hyun and current president Lee Myung-bak, found themselves to be the relentless target of opposition-based criticism from the beginning of their tenures and were under constant attack to delegitimize their respective leaderships. The most popular and perhaps easiest issue to target as the source for a wide range of public dissatisfaction is the alliance with the United States. In large part, this is because the alliance is more than just a joint-defense agreement; it has always been a political partnership as well, making it especially vulnerable to politicization by the public. The result has been the crippling of presidential power over issues such as the opening of the domestic beef market to American imports or the dispatch of troops to international missions in Iraq and Afghanistan. These issues are certainly related to the alliance, but they should have been debated publicly within the parameters of their respective issue areas and framed as a discussion of furthering national interests rather than implicating the alliance.

It is clear that President Lee, as well as the next leader of South Korea, will continue to confront public excoriation of his foreign policies, and that much of the criticism will attempt to draw linkages to the alliance. In the face of such a political environment, some have argued that one way to sustain public support for the alliance and build momentum toward the establishment of a broader partnership is to focus on the intrinsic, rather than merely the strategic, value of the alliance. For example, that the benefit of the alliance to the South Korean people is not derived just from the function of deterring North Korean aggression, but also from the very values and principles that the relationship stands for and pro-motes: democracy, open societies, and stability.

It is certainly critical to build a successful partnership based on the foundation of shared values—which should enhance the importance of the alliance as the partnership evolves—but it is not enough to fun-damentally alter a South Korean public mentality regarding national security that remains profoundly focused on peninsular concerns.[32] Although South Koreans have become more comfortable with the terminology of universal or global values and have incorporated their use in regular public discourse, an elemental, almost primordial chasm remains between what South Koreans can tangibly identify as imme-diate and imperative security interests—those that are local—and abstract goals and principles that are universal and therefore further removed from their national identity and interests.

To bridge this divide and encourage South Koreans to embrace inter-national goals and values in concrete terms, South Korean leadership needs to convince the public that these are integral to their own national interests rather than only indirectly relevant. American leadership can do its part through close cooperation with its partner to provide a unified rationale for how the alliance plays a pivotal role in preserving the entirety of national interest—not just peninsular, but regional and global as well. The most acceptable paradigm may be to frame the alli-ance not as the objective goal toward which national interests should be directed, but rather as the most effective means of achieving them over the long term. Furthermore, this framework should be able to articu-late future scenarios long past unification of the peninsula. Such a shift can likely be achieved only gradually and over the medium to long term. In the interim, the two governments should at a minimum endeavor to protect the alliance from any further damage or erosion.

In implementing activities, such as PKOs, that extend South Korea's reach to regional and global areas, the ROK government will have to manage more than just a fractious domestic audience at home. The government will be increasingly challenged by the proliferation of South Korean nongovernmental organizations (NGOs) and their growing involvement in multilateral activities overseas, such as disaster relief and humanitarian assistance missions. These groups often act outside the purview of governmental oversight and are at times either oblivious to dangerous conditions or purposefully ignore them.[33] This can often lead to disastrous consequences and seriously complicate national policy, as was seen in Afghanistan in 2007. On the other hand, they may play surprisingly positive roles, as they did in Haiti, by raising public sympathy for a humanitarian disaster. Thus, the government must find ways to work more closely with NGOs to find areas of strategic overlap in missions and goals.

IMPLICATIONS FOR THE ALLIANCE

In June 2009, the United States and the ROK adopted a Joint Vision for the Alliance, which provides a future-oriented blueprint for the development of the bilateral relationship. In the statement, the two allies pledge to "build a comprehensive strategic alliance of bilateral, regional and global scope, based on common values and mutual trust." In addition, the document specifically states that "the Alliance will enhance coordination on peacekeeping" as well as make other development and postconflict stabilization efforts.[34]

This vision statement is an extraordinary achievement given the tense period in the alliance that characterized the last decade. Yet it reflects not only the concerted efforts by both allies invested in reformulating and strengthening the formal alliance relationship, but also a growing convergence between the United States and the ROK on their global strategic outlooks. This is a welcome development, but it is also a necessary requirement for any further transformation of the alliance. A shared global strategy alone is insufficient, however, because it is fraught with the potential to bring to the fore two perennial concerns that have haunted the alliance since its inception: fear of abandonment on the one hand and entrapment on the other.[35]

As the United States turns more and more to its regional allies for support of global missions and the ROK becomes increasingly responsible for its own defense, this twin dynamic of paradoxical fears, in which South Korea is left to stand alone against the North or is forced to become involved in military conflicts off the peninsula, becomes even more compelling and plausible. These fears can be allayed only when South Koreans are able to fully embrace and support their country's indispensable role in contributing to security beyond the Korean peninsula, and view the alliance as an effective means to do so. ROK participation in PKOs may be a useful vehicle for demonstrating this new role.

CONCLUSION

The task for South Korean leaders is to make a strong case to the public that robust South Korean participation in PKOs unequivocally serves the national interest and benefits the country. It affords the opportunity to channel one of South Korea's strongest comparative advantages—human resource capital—toward contributing to an important global security issue and reinforces international recognition of a global Korea. It also benefits the maintenance of a vibrant economy that will continue its reliance on international markets for its strength.

The U.S.-ROK alliance undoubtedly has played a critical role in ensuring stability on the Korean peninsula and northeast Asia for the last half century. As the world confronts a vastly different security environment than the Cold War within which that alliance was born, the question for U.S. and ROK policymakers is how best to transform the current and existing functions of the unique security relationship to address twenty-first-century issues. The critical need for peacekeeping operations will only increase in the future, making this the ideal area for expansion. At the same time, South Korea's rapid modernization and development in the past few decades has propelled the country's international status and advanced its military capabilities to world-class levels.

But even as the ROK has the sixth-largest military in the world, its contributions to international peacekeeping and stabilization operations remain comparatively limited, as is the case for the other countries of Asia. Indeed, based on the size of militaries and economies in the Asia region, there is considerable peacekeeping capabilities in the area that are not being fully utilized. Despite its middle-power status, South Korea can play a unique leadership role in the global community by actively increasing its support for and participation in peacekeeping missions around the world.

President Lee has led his country on a bold and ambitious future path that envisions dramatically altering South Korea's international role, and PKOs offer an ideal way to realize these goals. Moreover, a joint vision for the future direction of the bilateral alliance calls for the transformation of the relationship into a true partnership that can address not just peninsular, but regional and global security concerns. Increased South Korean commitment to PKOs would serve to cement ROK commitment to this goal as well. Although it will not be an easy task, with careful coordination and management, South Korea has the potential to make a significant contribution to international stability and in so doing, enhance its security at home. The bilateral effort to find areas of cooperation not only ensures that the U.S.-ROK alliance is a unique and special relationship worthy of continued investment and commitment, but also intimately serves both countries' national and strategic interests, making it a necessary endeavor.

South Korea's Counterpiracy Operations in the Gulf of Aden

Terence Roehrig

In March 2009, the South Korean National Assembly approved the first foreign deployment of South Korea's naval forces to join the U.S.-led Combined Task Force (CTF-151). The purpose of CTF-151 is to conduct antipiracy operations in the Gulf of Aden and off Somalia's east coast by the Horn of Africa. South Korea joined the navies of twenty-four other countries that participate in the Combined Maritime Forces (CMF) through one of three combined task forces, CTF-150, CTF-151, and CTF-152, to help ensure maritime security in this region. The CMF is an international effort to conduct maritime security operations in the Gulf of Aden, the Arabian Sea, and the Indian Ocean.

South Korea has been a regular participant in CTF-151 with the important contribution of a destroyer, a helicopter, and special operations personnel to counterpiracy efforts in the region.[1] The Lee Myung-bak administration's most immediate concern has been the security of South Korea's commercial fleet and its citizens who work on shipping and fishing vessels, as it has seen an increasing number of its ships seized with demands for ever-higher ransoms. As a rising middle power with increasing economic and political clout, Seoul has assisted in a multilateral effort of the world's chief naval powers to address the challenge of piracy. Participation in CTF-151 and other international security initiatives has elevated the Republic of Korea's (ROK) status and reputation in the international community. Moreover, participation in these counterpiracy operations has provided valuable operational experience for its navy as a sole operator and in missions with international partners. The ROK navy has considerable experience to share with partners, given the work it must do for peninsular security, but these operations have also been able to improve these skills as well as the navy's ability to coordinate operations with others.

South Korea's participation in counterpiracy efforts in the Gulf of Aden has been a valuable venture undertaken at a relatively tolerable cost. Some analysts have argued that it needs to increase its involvement by sending one or two more ships. Seoul, however, should be reluctant to commit any further resources to these efforts at this time, given the serious security concerns it has to address closer to home with the North Korean threat. South Korean leaders will need to reconcile concerns regarding the serious defense challenges they face close to home and those in more distant oceans. South Korea's rising power and stature compel Seoul to contribute to the international efforts to bring security to the maritime commons. Indeed, the ROK has important interests to protect in foreign and domestic areas and must coordinate both without introducing unacceptable risk in either one.

However, the history of the task force begins several years earlier.

PIRACY AND SOUTH KOREA'S DECISION TO JOIN CTF-151

South Korean fishing and commercial vessels have a significant presence in the region, and as piracy increased, ROK ships traveling off the coast of Somalia also became more vulnerable. Approximately 29 percent of South Korea's maritime commerce traverses this region off the Somali coast; an estimated five hundred South Korean ships pass through the Gulf of Aden annually, and approximately one hundred and fifty of these are highly vulnerable to pirate attack because of their slow speed.[2]

In 2006, Somali pirates hijacked two tuna boats owned by the South Korean company Dongwon Fisheries. The crew of twenty-five that included eight South Koreans was released after four months of captivity for a ransom of close to $800,000. In May 2007, pirates seized two more ROK ships with four South Koreans on a crew of twenty-four. The ship was held for six months and released after paying another sizable, though undisclosed, ransom.

In 2008, piracy in the Gulf of Aden, including incidents involving ROK ships and citizens, escalated further. In May, pirates hijacked two fishing boats with a crew of twenty-five from Daechang Fisheries, releasing them six months later. In September, another South Korean vessel was hijacked with eight South Korean crew members on board. This ship was released after being held for a month. Finally, in November 2008, pirates seized a Japanese freighter, the twenty-thousand-ton

Chemstar Venus, with five South Koreans in a crew of twenty-three. The ship was released in April 2009, but it was not clear whether a ransom was paid.

With piracy on the rise off the coast of Somalia, on June 2, 2008, the United Nations Security Council (UNSC) passed Resolution 1816 unanimously with the consent of Somalia's transition government that provided authorization to use "all necessary means" to "enter the territorial waters of Somalia for the purpose of repressing acts of piracy and armed robbery at sea, in a manner consistent with such action permitted on the high seas with respect to piracy under relevant international law."[3] In October 2008, UNSC Resolution 1838 requested specific assistance from "states interested in the security of maritime activities" to assist "by deploying naval vessels and military aircraft, in accordance with international law."[4] Since then, the UNSC has passed three resolutions, 1897 (2009), 1950 (2010), and 2020 (2011), to reauthorize the UN mandate to continue counterpiracy operations in the region for another twelve months.[5] Ironically, because the Somali government has granted permission for the operations, the UN Security Council resolutions are technically unnecessary. However, UN approval provides important political cover and is necessary for some states to commit military forces to an international operation.[6]

To implement these UN resolutions, states agreed in January 2009 to form CTF-151. As piracy incidents mounted and UNSC resolutions called for an international response, the cabinet at the Blue House approved a plan to send a naval unit to participate in international counterpiracy operations in January 2009, and the National Assembly approved the motion in early March. The unit was named *Cheonghae* for a naval base established by General Jang Bogo during the Silla dynasty to protect the kingdom's commercial ships and coastal population from pirates.[7] While ROK leaders were considering a final decision, a team of navy and foreign ministry officials inspected the facilities in the region and Commander Choi Soo-yong at the Joint Staff concluded that "conditions at the port of Djibouti, in Bahrain and other support situations there were quite good. There will be no problem regarding logistics support because we can use the services of local companies contracted with other navies, such as the United States, Britain and Germany."[8] South Korea was now set to deploy naval forces away from the Korean peninsula for the first time in its history.

ROK NAVAL CAPABILITY

An important prerequisite for participation in a multilateral maritime operation of this sort is to possess the necessary naval capability. It was particularly important to have blue-water assets that could deploy long distances and operate in the open ocean. In March 2001, President Kim Dae-jung declared in a speech to the graduating class of the Korean Naval Academy that South Korea would pursue the development of a blue-water navy with a "strategic mobile fleet that protects state interests in the five big oceans and plays a role of keeping peace in the world."[9] In March 2008, Defense Minister Lee Sang-hee delivered a statement from President Lee Myung-bak to another graduating class at the academy, emphasizing the importance of naval power for South Korea's interests:

> The 21st century is the era of the ocean. We have to build a state-of-the-art force that can protect our maritime sovereignty. With a vision for an advanced deep-sea Navy, our Navy should become a force that can ensure the security of maritime transportation lines, and contribute to peace in the world. Sea is the turf for our survival and national prosperity. Only if we efficiently defend and use the sea can peace and economic growth be secured.[10]

As a result, South Korea embarked on a major ship-building effort to develop an ocean-going navy under the banner "To the Sea, to the World."

The effort began with a three-phase construction program to build destroyers. The first phase was the development of the *Gwanggaeto the Great*–class DDH-I light destroyers, the first of which was commissioned in 1998.[11] At 3,800 tons each, the ships are considered by some to be in the smaller frigate class. The DDH-I destroyers are configured for strike operations, antisubmarine warfare (ASW), screening and convoy duty, and support for amphibious operations. Ships of this class are capable of carrying two helicopters, but space is tight to realistically deploy with both.

Central to South Korea's participation in CTF-151 has been its fleet of DDH-II destroyers, the *Chungmugong Yi Sunshin*–class ships. The first of these vessels, the namesake of the class, was commissioned in 2003 with additional vessels commissioned each year through 2008. South Korea's DDH-II destroyers and the dates in which they were commissioned are presented in Figure 2.

FIGURE 2. SOUTH KOREA'S DDH-II DESTROYERS

	Ship	Commissioned
DDH 975	Chungmugong Yi Sunshin	2003
DDH 976	Munmu the Great	2004
DDH 977	Daejoyoung	2005
DDH 978	Wang Geon	2006
DDH 979	Kang Gam-chan	2007
DDH 981	Choi Young	2008

The DDH-II is a 4,500-ton stealth destroyer with a hull design capable of deflecting radar and possessing other antidetection techniques. The ship is equipped with top-level combat systems that include advanced air defense and antisubmarine warfare capabilities, Harpoon ship-to-ship missiles, RAM MK-31 ship-to-ship guided missiles, and the Goalkeeper system for antiship torpedoes and missiles. DDH-II destroyers are also built to function as the command ship in a combat task force. For deployment to CTF-151, the DDH-II was well suited in that it had a helicopter deck and storage facilities capable of handling two Lynx helicopters. The Lynx helicopter is a multipurpose platform and crucial for counterpiracy operations. It can carry a team of sea, air, and land (SEAL) personnel and other weapons systems to reach targets more quickly, which greatly extends the reach and response time of the destroyer. The DDH-II was also constructed with extra berthing space to accommodate additional personnel, such as the SEAL teams that are part of the *Cheonghae* unit.

The third phase of South Korea's destroyer program was the construction of the DDH-III Aegis-class destroyer, *King Sejong the Great*. The ship is a 7,600-ton multipurpose vessel equipped with the latest technology, including SPY-1D radar that can track close to nine hundred targets and engage seventeen of them simultaneously. The ship also has advanced torpedo- and missile-launching systems, an antiair and antimissile defense system more advanced than the Phalanx Close-In Weapons System (CIWS), and an advanced anti-ballistic missile system to deal with North Korea's ballistic missile threat. In addition to the *King Sejong the Great*, Seoul has built and commissioned two other Aegis-class ships, *Yulgok Yi I* and *Seoae Yu Seong-ryong*, and has plans to build others.

ANTIPIRACY OPERATIONS IN THE GULF OF ADEN

In March 2009, South Korea deployed the *Cheonghae* unit for the first time to operations in the Gulf of Aden. (A complete list of South Korean DDH deployments as part of CTF-151 is presented in Figure 3.) The deployment consisted of one DDH-II destroyer, the *Munmu the Great*, under the command of Commander Jang Sung-woo with a crew of three hundred that included thirty ROK SEALs, along with a Lynx helicopter. ROK naval officials planned on rotating the DDH-II destroyers every six months.

The *Cheonghae* unit conducts weekly convoys, largely for South Korean ships traveling through the Gulf of Aden, and participates in other CTF-151 operations. Despite these efforts, the ROK warship is able to accompany only 13 percent of South Korean vessels that pass through the region.[12] Yet, during the first thirty months of operations in the region, South Korean forces rescued ten civilian vessels.[13]

The South Korean force operates under a bifurcated chain of command reporting first to the ROK Joint Staff and ROK navy headquarters but with loose tactical control by the leadership of CTF-151. The *Cheonghae* commander's first priority is to protect ROK vessels that traverse the Gulf of Aden. Based on shipping schedules provided by the ROK Joint Staff, the ROK DDH commander knows which South Korean commercial ships are passing through the Internationally Recommended Transit Corridor and escorts them on this journey. If no South Korean ships are scheduled, the coalition staff of CTF-151 will direct the ship to proceed to a particular sector of the IRTC for an open patrol, or sweep mission, to protect any ships within the sector from pirate attacks. If an attack should occur during an open patrol, the *Cheonghae* commander contacts the ROK Joint Staff and ROK navy headquarters, with simultaneous notification to CTF-151 staff. To act, the ROK commander must first receive authorization from ROK command authority at the joint staff and navy. If there are no other competing priorities to protect ROK ships or people, permission is likely to be granted. Then, should the ROK warship be the closest and best asset to send to the impending operation, CTF-151 will assume a coordination role to direct the ROK ship or other CTF-151 assets to the area.

Soon after arriving in the region, the *Munmu the Great* conducted several rescue operations. One of the most interesting was the rescue of a North Korean iron-ore freighter, the *Dabaksol*, a 6,400-ton vessel en route to India from the Red Sea. On May 4, 2009, the Democratic People's Republic of Korea ship was chased by pirates and sent out a distress call. The ship was located about twenty-three miles south of Aden, the chief port in Yemen. According to Captain Jang, the ROK ship had twenty to thirty minutes to reach the vessel if it hoped to prevent capture. The ship dispatched its Lynx helicopter and a team of snipers, which arrived within five minutes. The pirates decided to flee when the snipers began preparations to fire. Captain Jang remarked, "South Korea's navy is trained for a quick response, including routine antispy drills. Training continued while we were on the move, and I think the exercises paid off because of our efficiency and speedy response."[14]

Later in the month, the *Munmu the Great* chased off a pirate ship pursuing an Egyptian vessel on its way to India. Similar to the *Dabaksol* operation, the *Cheonghae* unit sent out its Lynx helicopter and a team of snipers to chase away the pirate craft. A U.S. Navy helicopter also joined the effort, making this the first joint operation with the United States since South Korea joined CTF-151. It was also the fourth rescue operation conducted by the *Cheonghae* unit since it arrived in April, the vessel having rescued Danish and Panamanian ships in addition to the *Dabaksol*.[15] On returning from his deployment, Captain Jang noted that "allied forces gave high marks to the Korean navy's capabilities and assigned us the most pirate-infested area of northern Bosaso off Somalia. We are proud to raise South Korea's reputation in the international community."[16]

The *Cheonghae* unit faced another difficult task in spring 2010. On April 4, the 300,000-ton ROK supertanker *Samho Dream* was hijacked 932 miles southeast of the Gulf of Aden. The ship was not under escort at the time, believing that it was traveling in waters relatively safe from piracy. The tanker was carrying two million barrels of crude oil, worth $160 million to $170 million, and was bound for the United States from Iraq with a crew of five South Koreans and nineteen Filipinos. Because of the nature of the cargo, crew members did not carry weapons. After receiving the hijack report, ROK authorities dispatched the ROK's *Yi Sunshin*, the DDH-II destroyer assigned to the *Cheonghae* unit at the time. The *Yi Sunshin* intercepted the hijacked vessel in two days but kept its distance. The pirates warned the destroyer to stay away, and when the pirates began negotiating with the ship's owner, the Busan-based Samho Shipping Company, the destroyer pulled back and returned to port.[17] After more than seven months of captivity, the *Samho Dream* and its crew were released for a $9.5 million ransom. According to a Reuters report, the pirates had initially demanded $20 million but settled for the lesser amount, which was a record for a ship's ransom paid in the region.[18] Before this incident, the highest ransom paid for an oil tanker had been $5.5 million. According to another report, though the ROK government did not provide the ransom money, the Lee administration viewed the events as a national embarrassment that signaled the country's weakness to deal with these situations, a particularly stinging indictment in the wake of the *Yeonpyeong* incident.[19]

On April 21, 2010, South Korea assumed command of CTF-151 under the lead of Rear Admiral (RADM) Lee Beom-rim, the first time Seoul led a CMF task force. During his tenure, RADM Lee sought to improve coordination with the EU and NATO contingents, along with other states that had naval assets present in the region but operated independently of any of the international task forces. On September 1, 2010, South Korea turned command responsibility over to Turkey. RADM Lee remarked:

> The Republic of Korea Navy is proud to have been at the forefront of CMF's efforts to help to confront piracy over the last four months. The men and women from twenty-one ships from seven different countries who have served under my command have performed their duties with skill and dedication.... It is important for us to share the latest strategic operations and tactical knowledge and I believe that we have worked seamlessly together toward our mutual goals.[20]

South Korea took the lead of CTF-151 a second time on June 18, 2012, when Rear Admiral Chung An-ho assumed command of the task force.

FIGURE 3. SOUTH KOREA'S DDH DEPLOYMENTS TO CTF-151

Ship	Dates Deployed
Munmu the Great	March–July 2009
Daejoyoung	July–November 2009
Chungmugong Yi Sunshin	November 2009–May 2010
Kang Gam-chan	May–September 2010
Wang Geon	September–December 2010
Choi Young	December 2010–May 2011
Chungmugong Yi Sunshin	May–November 2011
Munmu the Great	November 2011–May 2012
Wang Geon	May 2012–

He will lead a staff of twenty officers from South Korea, the United States, the Netherlands, Thailand, Jordan, Turkey, and Saudi Arabia.

The *Cheonghae* unit made a particularly good accounting of itself on January 21, 2011, when a detachment of twenty-one ROK SEALs rescued the 11,500-ton chemical carrier *Samho Jewelry*, owned by Samho Shipping, the same owner as the *Samho Dream*. (A map of the areas where the hijacking and rescue occurred are presented in Figure 4.) The drama began on January 15, when Somali pirates seized the *Samho Jewelry* in waters between India and Oman. The following day, the ROK's *Choi Young*, the DDH-II on duty at the time, was sent to the area and eventually caught up with the *Samho Jewelry* in the evening hours. Soon after, a Mongolian ship passed within eleven kilometers of the hijacked ship and four pirates boarded a small boat that headed toward the ship. With the pirates separated, ROK authorities decided to act. The Lynx helicopter went after the small boat and killed all four pirates on board. At the same time, a ten-member SEAL detachment traveled by speedboat to overtake the pirates on board the *Samho Jewelry*. As the SEALs approached the ship, the pirates opened fire, wounding three of the commandos and foiling the rescue attempt. The SEALs received medical treatment for non-life-threatening injuries and were flown to Oman for further treatment.[21]

During this rescue attempt, ROK officers on the *Choi Young* realized the pirates were not heavily armed and later attempted to negotiate

FIGURE 4

Map of the Samho rescue mission

Source: http://www.seanews.com.tr/article/PIRACY/49738/South-Korea-Piracy-Navy-Samho--Jewelry/.

with them. However, the *Samho Jewelry* began moving again, most likely toward Somali waters. With few options remaining, the SEALs on the *Choi Young* struck again. With the ROK warship providing covering fire, the SEALs attacked and retook control of the ship in a five-hour operation that required them to move cabin by cabin to root out the pirates.[22] Code-named Gulf of Aden Daybreak, the assault freed the ship's crew of twenty-one with none of them killed and only the *Samho Jewelry*'s captain wounded. The *Samho* captain, Seok Hae-kyun, later received the Dongbaek Medal, a civilian award for bravery in recognition of his actions during the ordeal. Eight of the thirteen Somali pirates on board were killed in the operation; five were captured and bound for trial in South Korea.

After the operation, South Koreans collectively swelled with pride over the *Cheonghae* unit's success. ROK minister of foreign affairs and trade Kim Sung-hwan noted, "It would be troubling to give the pirates money so easily. They must realize that South Korea isn't so soft."[23] In nationally televised remarks, President Lee Myung-bak proclaimed, "This operation demonstrated our government's strong will that we won't tolerate illegal activities by pirates anymore."[24] Regarding the navy's performance, President Lee exclaimed, "Our military flawlessly carried out the mission under difficult circumstances."[25] The successful rescue operation also had important political implications. After criticism for a relatively tepid response to the shelling of *Yeonpyeongdo*, one commentator noted that the president "could ill-afford the public percep-tion of a leader afraid to fight back."[26] The successful raid helped boost the reputation of the ROK navy and support for the Lee administration.

In the wake of the rescue operation and impressed with South Korea's response, the United Arab Emirates (UAE) asked for ROK assistance to train its special forces in counterpiracy operations. In July 2011, Seoul sent ten SEALs to provide the training. South Korea already had a con-tingent of 130 special operations personnel in the UAE since January 2011 for counterterrorism training and joint operations. Because the original authorization was for 150, adding ten more did not exceed the legislative mandate and did not require National Assembly approval.[27]

After the rescue operation, ROK authorities transported the five captured Somali pirates back to South Korea for trial in the Busan District Court. All five were convicted by a South Korean jury and received sentences that included life in prison for the pirate who had shot the Samho Jewelry captain. The others received sentences that ranged from thirteen to fifteen years in prison. Few countries have chosen to prosecute hijackers for piracy, and the trial attracted inter-national attention.[28] The Somali pirates appealed their sentences, and the Busan appellate court upheld the convictions, but most of the sentences, including the life sentence, were reduced. However, in Sep-tember 2011, it was announced that the case would be heard by the South Korean Supreme Court for a final decision, though the case has yet to be heard.[29] Prosecuting captured pirates has been a difficult task given the legal and jurisdictional issues. Consequently, approximately nine out of ten have been released.[30] In 2009, for example, ROK forces captured seven pirates in a rescue operation of a Bahamian freighter but released them after giving them warnings.[31]

Although many praised the rescue operation, critics also expressed concerns. In particular, some worried for other ROK hostages still held by pirates or any future captives. In a phone interview with Reuters after the Samho Jewelry raid, a Somali pirate warned, "We never planned to kill but now we shall seek revenge. We shall never take a ransom from South Korean ships; we shall burn them and kill their crew. We shall redouble our efforts. South Korea has put itself in trouble by killing my colleagues."[32] Indicating that the operation may have been more about politics, a South Korean professor lamented, "It's been a cam-paign to get credit from voters. The government should be more con-cerned about the hostages still out there. What is it doing for them? The reaction to the rescue should have been more muted."[33]

Another incident involving a South Korean vessel was the hijacking of the *Keummi* 305, also known as the *Golden Wave* No. 305, a 241-ton fishing trawler taken by pirates off the Somali coast in October 2010. The crew of forty-three was composed of two South Koreans, two Chinese, and thirty-nine Kenyans; some feared these captives would be the target of the pirates' revenge. There was also some intense discussion among ROK officials about arranging a swap for the crew of the *Golden Wave* for the five pirates captured in the *Samho Jewelry* rescue. The foreign ministry rejected the plan, however, most likely based on a refusal to negotiate with the pirates.[34] Three weeks after the *Samho Jewelry* assault, the pirates released the ship with the crew unharmed and no ransom paid. According to one report, it appeared that the pirates released the ship because it was becoming exceedingly unlikely that any ransom would be paid for such a small ship, one owned by the ship captain rather than a large shipping firm. Moreover, feeding the crew of forty-three was becoming difficult.[35]

The *Cheonghae* unit continued to contribute to maritime security following the successful rescue of the *Samho Jewelry*. Early on April 21, 2011, Somali pirates fired small arms at the 75,000-ton container ship, the *Hanjin Tianjin*, owned by the ROK Hanjin Shipping Company. The captain of the vessel sent out a distress call and ordered the engines shut down. The crew proceeded to lock itself inside the citadel, an emergency, bullet-proof panic room for protection during pirate attacks. In February, the Ministry of Land, Transport and Maritime Affairs had mandated all commercial vessels traveling through the region to install a citadel and an independent communications system within the room.[36] Though the *Hanjin Tianjin* had the citadel, it had not installed the communications system. ROK authorities immediately dispatched the *Choi Young* to the ship's aid. However, a Turkish warship only eighty miles away was able to reach the *Hanjin Tianjin* eight and a half hours sooner and may have also played a role in chasing away the pirates. Apparently, the pirates had vanished by the time the Turkish ship and later the *Choi Young* arrived, but shell casings and footprints from bare feet were evident on the ship, sure signs of the pirates' presence. It was also clear that the pirates had attempted to restart the engines but had failed. With the crew safe in the citadel and the ship immobile, the pirates left.[37]

In early July, the *Cheonghae* unit responded again to three pirate ships believed to be moving in to seize the 17,000-ton chemical freighter *Azalea,* owned by the ROK firm STX POS. The ship had a crew of twenty-four with four South Koreans and was carrying 28,000 tons of sulfur from Egypt to Singapore. The *Chungmugong Yi Sunshin* was escorting another vessel when the distress call arrived. As a result, the ROK warship transferred its mission to a nearby Spanish warship and steamed off to rescue the *Azalea.* When in range, the ROK warship dispatched its Lynx helicopter and upon reaching the pirate ships, the helicopter fired flares to warn the pirates. All three pirate ships sped off before the *Yi Sunshin* arrived.[38]

In addition to contributing to counterpiracy operations, the South Korean government has also provided financial support to UN counterpiracy efforts. In April 2011, Seoul provided $500,000 to a UN fund for the Contact Group on Piracy off the Coast of Somalia (CGPCS). As of November 2010, the fund had received $3.66 million from member countries.[39] The group was established by the UN in January 2009 following UNSC Resolution 1851 and maintains five working groups to address various dimensions of the piracy problem, including legal issues, information sharing, and financial dealings.[40] The CGPCS is a "voluntary, ad hoc international forum of approximately seventy countries, organizations and industry groups with a common interest in combating piracy in the Gulf of Aden and the Indian Ocean, and bringing to justice pirates and their financiers and facilitators."[41] At South Korea's suggestion, the group will also maintain a website operated jointly by South Korea, the United States, and the United Kingdom to act as an information-sharing and communications hub between the group members.

BENEFITS OF SOUTH KOREA'S COUNTERPIRACY EFFORTS

South Korea's participation in CTF-151 has yielded a number of benefits. First, the presence of the *Cheonghae* unit has helped protect both ROK commercial interests in the Gulf of Aden and Arabian Sea and its citizens involved in maritime commerce there. ROK warships have escorted many South Korean ships through the region and moved in to ward off pirate attacks. The most dramatic of these was the rescue of the *Samho Jewelry*. It is difficult to calculate in monetary terms the benefit of the *Cheonghae* unit's presence; but given South Korea's dependence on ocean-borne shipping, the approximately $33 million spent annually to fund the deployment is money well spent. The deployment also put an end to an apparent wave of ransom demands in which South Korean ships became priorities for the hijackers. According to one report, the high ransoms paid by ROK shipping companies, particularly the $9.5 million paid for the *Samho Dream*, may have singled out South Korean ships.[42]

As a rising middle power that depends heavily on the oceans to maintain its export-driven economy, South Korea bears some responsibility to help protect the global maritime commons. South Korea's assistance in these efforts provides an important boost to its international standing. Moreover, operations such as the *Samho Jewelry* rescue demonstrate that South Korea is willing and able to use force when necessary, making it a valued partner. As one analyst noted, "This incident has left a strong impression on countries in the region … that South Korea is not a paper tiger on the piracy issue and is willing and able to use hard power to protect its nationals and property."[43]

Finally, CTF-151 operations also have provided South Korea with a chance to share its operational experience gained through its preparation for North Korean actions, while also gaining from participating in and leading multilateral operations. Gulf of Aden actions provide the ROK navy with valuable operational experience. In addition, successful counterpiracy operations, especially the *Samho Jewelry*, may have helped to send a deterrence message to the pirates and North Korea, while allowing the navy and the Lee administration to redeem its reputation in the wake of the *Cheonan* sinking and the *Yeonpyeongdo* skirmish. However, it is unclear whether ROK counterpiracy operations had a significant deterrent effect and, if so, it is likely to be limited. The financial gain to be had in piracy in the Gulf of Aden and the difficulty of policing such a large area make deterring piracy a difficult task. The deterrent effect on North Korea may be slightly greater in that it was a demonstration of a more determined ROK government willing to use force in response to a future provocation. However, ROK efforts to aid North Korean ships in trouble in the Gulf of Aden may have had an even greater effect in softening inter-Korean relations; but in all these cases, it is difficult to ascertain the ultimate effect in Pyongyang.

QUESTIONS FOR THE FUTURE

The year 2012 marks the third year of ROK participation in CTF-151, and operations such as the dramatic rescue of the *Samho Jewelry* raise some important questions regarding South Korea's participation and the overall value of the venture for ROK interests. Three issues are of greatest concern: increasing the size of the *Cheonghae* unit, sustaining the cost and public support of the operation, and the use of force in rescue operations.

INCREASING THE SIZE OF THE CHEONGHAE UNIT

Some critics have argued that given the success of the ROK deployment and that other countries such as Japan, China, and the United States have sent larger contingents of two or three warships to fight piracy in the region, South Korea should deploy more ships as well. Moreover, given the size of the region and the ongoing threat of pirate attacks, more needs to be done to protect ROK shipping.

Although a reasonable idea, it would be difficult for South Korea to deploy other naval assets to the Gulf of Aden, given the size of its current force and its defense needs at home. One option would be to increase the *Cheonghae* unit from one to two *Chungmugong Yi Sunshin* DDH-II destroyers. Although South Korea has six ships in this class, and thus seemingly might be able to spare one more for antipiracy duty, such a conclusion is incorrect. Sending one DDH-II ship to the Gulf of Aden is equivalent to committing three ships. While one ship is conducting operations, another is either on its way to the theater and training for the mission or returning from a deployment. A third DDH-II would be in port, undergoing maintenance after the regular six-month deployment. Thus, the commitment of one destroyer to actual counterpiracy operations is really the commitment of three DDH-II vessels. Moreover, the remaining three destroyers in this class are needed for operations around the Korean peninsula, making it difficult to deploy more of these ships to the counterpiracy mission.

Other ships in the ROK fleet are not as suitable for antipiracy operations. The DDH-III *Aegis*-class destroyers are costly to deploy and not designed to be counterpiracy platforms. When South Korea began its commitment to CTF-151, the *King Sejong the Great* had only been recently commissioned and was still conducting training exercises.

Furthermore, these ships are more valuable for their ballistic missile defense capabilities against North Korea. The other possible additions to the *Cheonghae* unit are the DDH-I destroyers or the *Ulsan*-class frigates. However, deploying these to the Gulf of Aden is also problematic. The frigates are good for coastal patrol but do not have a helicopter deck. They are also too small to carry the extra SEAL teams and support personnel necessary for the operation. The DDH-I destroyers are equipped with a helicopter deck but lack the space to accommodate the additional personnel. Moreover, there are only three of these ships in the fleet, and they are needed for defense at home. One possible answer is the new *Incheon*-class frigate, but only one has been launched, and it will be a few years before others are available for service. Thus, it is unlikely that South Korea will be able to increase the size of the *Cheonghae* unit in the near term, but doing so could be part of a longer-range plan to combat piracy once more ships are constructed.

SUSTAINING THE COST AND SUPPORT OF THE CHEONGHAE UNIT

The annual cost of the *Cheonghae* unit deployment is approximately $33 million of a total $27.6 billion ROK defense budget.[44] The cost is relatively modest, one-tenth of 1 percent, but as with most governments in the midst of the global economic slowdown, budgets are tight and all line items are competing for scarce resources. In addition, ROK politics remain intensely divided, including support for the counterpiracy mission. However, the success of the *Samho Jewelry* operation seems to have tipped the scale somewhat; and at least for the moment, sufficient support remains for continuing ROK participation in the operation.

USE OF FORCE IN RESCUE OPERATIONS

Following the *Samho Jewelry* rescue, critics raised concerns that the use of deadly force had set a dangerous precedent that might make it an easier decision next time and could jeopardize the well-being of the hostages. Rescue operations are clearly dangerous, and there can be no guarantee that they will be free of casualties. These are important concerns, and authorities of any country should consider the circumstances and the likelihood of success carefully before ordering a rescue attempt. However, the addition of more measures—such as a citadel—would reduce the danger. If opportunities exist to rescue hostages from an uncertain fate, they should be considered. Nonetheless, successful rescue operations remain difficult and should be contemplated only reluctantly. It is therefore critical that seizures be prevented, which would reduce the need to conduct rescue operations in the first place.

CONCLUSION

Counterpiracy operations are one part of a solution to address a problem that is rooted in a lack of effective governance and poverty.[45] These dimensions will need to be addressed as well for any hope of a more permanent solution. Increasingly, transnational challenges like piracy will require multilateral solutions such as CTF-151. ROK participation in these efforts helps to provide greater global security and advance South Korean interests. Moreover, as South Korea's power and influence in the international system increases, it will be incumbent on Seoul to play a proportionate role in providing security for the global commons. Participation in CTF-151 is an important contribution South Korea should make as a rising power to help address transnational challenges.

The ROK Provincial Reconstruction Team in Afghanistan

John Hemmings

Following the terrorist attacks on New York on September 11, 2001, South Korean president Kim Dae-jung declared a "support policy" for U.S. overseas operations on September 24, 2001, and authorized the deployment of Republic of Korea (ROK) troops to Afghanistan on December 7, 2001. In taking this action, Kim Dae-jung responded in the spirit of the alliance—South Korea is not obliged to deploy its forces for America's defense in the U.S.-ROK Mutual Defense Treaty—with a tangible contribution to an operation far from Korean borders where its U.S. ally was responding to an enemy attack. By February 2002, sixty medics from the Dong-eui Medical Unit arrived in Afghanistan, where they established a South Korean field hospital at Bagram Airfield (BAF). The following year, 150 engineers from the Dasan Engineering Unit were also deployed to BAF, and were tasked with carrying out the construction and expansion of the base facilities. Although South Korea's contributions in Afghanistan were small, there was still some uneasiness within South Korea regarding the deployment of South Korean personnel to a mission not connected with South Korea's immediate security interests.

South Korea's small medical detachment and engineering unit contributions received little public attention until two incidents in 2007 tested South Korea's willingness to commit resources to stability in Afghanistan. In February 2007, a South Korean soldier was killed in a suicide bombing at a BAF gate, and in July of that year twenty-three South Korean Christian missionaries were taken hostage by the Taliban on the road from Kandahar to Kabul. Although two of the hostages were executed, the South Korean government negotiated the release of the remaining twenty-one hostages in return for pledges to withdraw the South Korean deployment scheduled for later that year. This seeming retreat in the face of demands by the insurgents, alongside the Taliban claim that a ransom of $20 million had been paid, seemed to damage South Korea's standing with the United States and other allies involved in fighting in Afghanistan.[1]

However, in 2008 South Korea returned to Afghanistan, building a hospital and training center on Bagram Airfield. Building on the success of this project, South Korea decided to subsequently deploy a full-scale provincial reconstruction team (PRT), near Bagram, in Parwan Province. This unlikely South Korean contribution, following South Korea's earlier withdrawal from Afghanistan in 2007, is evidence of South Korean staying power as an international contributor to security beyond South Korea's immediate neighborhood.

EVOLUTION OF PROVINCIAL RECONSTRUCTION TEAMS IN AFGHANISTAN

Following the downfall of the Taliban in 2001 and the resulting Bonn Agreement, the International Security Assistance Force (ISAF) was created to help establish the authority of the nascent Afghan government in all thirty-four provinces of Afghanistan. In late 2001, the U.S. government created the PRT model, to carry out three objectives: improve security, extend the authority of the government in Kabul, and facilitate reconstruction in the province. Initially, small groups of ten to twelve military personnel were created—called Coalition Humanitarian Liaison Cells. These groups were tasked with implementing small Department of Defense (DOD)–funded projects.[2] Then, in February 2003, the U.S. embassy in Afghanistan issued a general set of parameters in a document titled *Principles Guiding PRT Working Relations with UNAMA, NGOs and Local Government*, which developed the PRT concept by adding a force-protection component and a variety of civil and military expertise.[3] This blend of civil and military operations is revealed in the personnel chosen to operate the PRTs. Although U.S. PRTs, for example, are commanded and staffed mostly by DOD personnel, they also have staff from the Department of State (DOS), the U.S. Agency for International Development (USAID), and the Department of Agriculture (USDA), who together make up the leadership team of each PRT. Due to the military commander's control over security decisions, budgeting, and much of the base personnel and resources, they tend to be a "first among equals." PRTs in Afghanistan are ultimately under ISAF operational command, but individual nations, including South Korea, decide on how the PRTs they lead are staffed and run. The command structure under which PRTs operate in Afghanistan is shown in Figure 5.

SOUTH KOREA AND STABILIZATION

In July 2009, U.S. secretary of defense Robert M. Gates traveled to South Korea and Japan to request support for U.S. operations in Afghanistan.[4] On October 30, the ROK government announced plans

FIGURE 5

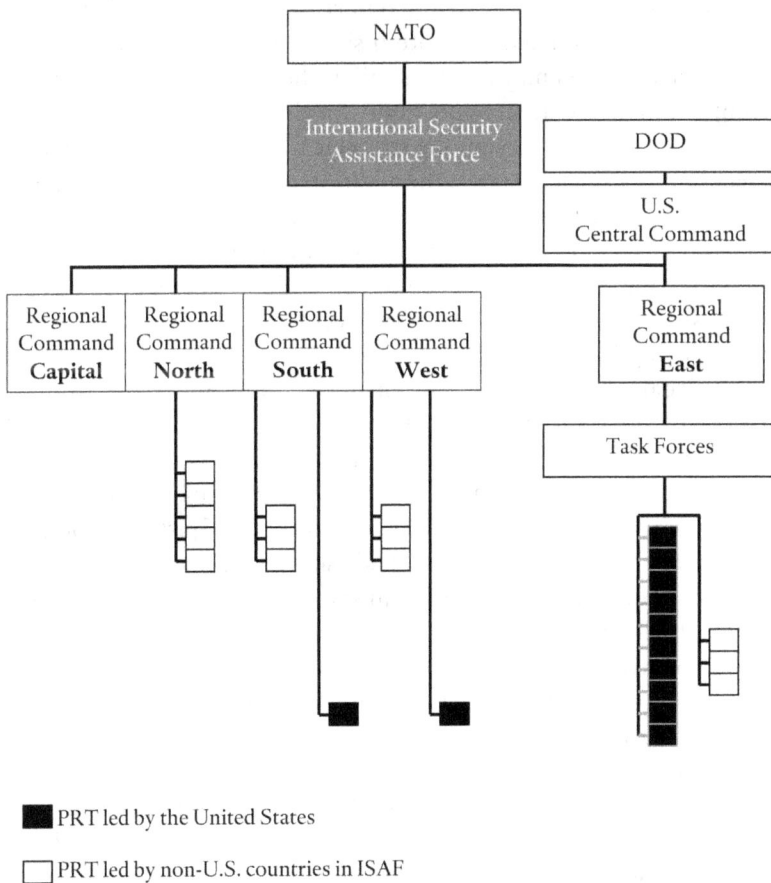

![Figure 5 organizational chart]

- PRT led by the United States
- PRT led by non-U.S. countries in ISAF

Source: GAO analysis of ISAF and Department of Defense data.

to establish an ROK-run provincial reconstruction team near Chari-kar, the capital of Parwan Province, where the team would take over from a U.S. PRT operating from Bagram Airfield. The commencement of the ROK PRT in Parwan marks a turning point in South Korea's overseas deployment policy, giving the ROK armed forces and civilian actors their first opportunity to take part in stabilization operations in a coordinated fashion.

Although South Korea has a strong history of peacekeeping activi-ties, stabilization is different from traditional peacekeeping opera-tions in that there is not yet a peace to keep, and development work, the provision of security, and counterinsurgency take place side by side, carried out by a mixture of civilian and military actors.[5] As explained in a United Kingdom government report, "humanitarian, develop-ment and stabilization activities often share operational 'space.' But although the activities may appear similar, the guiding principles are different."[6] This presents an opportunity for closer cooperation within the U.S.-ROK alliance, serving the strategic needs and values of both partners. For the United States, the addition of ROK capabilities and resources is an added bonus in a time of financial austerity and tighten-ing budgets. As some U.S. policy analysts have pointed out, carrying out stabilization alongside U.S. forces gives South Korean agencies and forces capabilities that might prove necessary in postcollapse sce-narios involving North Korea.[7]

On February 25, 2010, the National Assembly of South Korea approved the deployment of the PRT team of 336 personnel[8] to the new facilities outside of the provincial capital of Charikar (population fifty-four thousand) in Parwan Province.[9] Parwan Province is one of Afghanistan's smaller provinces, with a population of just 560,000 in the central region, and until recently had escaped much of the fighting that has wracked other parts of Afghanistan. Located thirty-five miles to the north of Kabul, it has become a source of agricultural produce for Kabul markets as well as a center for provincial trade. From 2009 to 2010, Parwan produced more than 91,000 tons of wheat, making it the largest supplier in the central region provinces.[10] Ethnically, the prov-ince is divided among Tajiks, Pashtuns, Uzbeks, Qizilbash, Kuchi, and Hazaras. During the 1990s, it was part of the Northern Alliance territory under Ahmad Shah Massoud's control. Because the province straddled the border between Taliban-controlled and Massoud-controlled terri-tory, it saw some of the heaviest fighting between the Northern Alliance and Taliban in 2001. Certain districts, particularly those with Pashtun majorities, continue to have security issues.[11] In August 2010, a suicide squad of six Taliban attacked Governor Abdul Basir Salangi's mansion in Charikar, killing twenty-two and wounding thirty-four.[12] The following month, two German aid workers were killed near the Salang Pass, though their killers remain unknown.[13] Despite these recent incidents, the province has a safe reputation overall.

Named the Ashna Unit (*ashna* means friend in Dari), the unit reports to a task force based at Regional Command East at Bagram Airfield and is commanded by a senior civilian, a diplomat from the Ministry of Foreign Affairs and Trade. In addition to this representative, the Korea International Cooperation Agency (KOICA) and the Ministry of National Defense (MND) are also represented in the PRT by a KOICA director and an army colonel, as well as a representative of the South Korean police force. The civilian component of the South Korean PRT is quite large: eleven KOICA staff members and eight Afghan teachers for the Educational and Cultural Center. There are also fifty police trainers, who work both on the base and at Bagram Air Field. The civilian component works on a range of different areas, including medical aid, governance, education and vocational training, and agricultural development.

In addition to the development team, the PRT also has a sizable military contingent, which is composed of five military teams: headquarters staff, security/escort teams, air support, tactical support, and a diplomatic escort.[14] The four functions of the military team include protection of the base, protection of PRT staff when moving around the local area, air travel, and support functions. This last area is composed of logistics, supply, and communications. On June 30, 2011, the United States handed over formal responsibility for more than seventy-five local projects to South Korea.[15] Despite this handover of responsibility, however, U.S. personnel continued to play a role. For the first two months, for example, ROK and U.S. forces carried out joint patrols of the area. This day-to-day work was aided by the decision to incorporate a small number of U.S. Forces Korea (USFK) personnel within the Ashna staff. This U.S. group, in addition to and including U.S. personnel of South Korean descent, was able to help with cultural and language barriers to cooperation, which they had experience with from their time in Korea or growing up.[16]

The PRT set four areas of focus for its project work: governance, medical aid, education/vocation, and agricultural development.

GOVERNANCE

– The PRT established the Police Training Center (PTC) at the base in Charikar. With eight police trainers, the PTC provides training in tae kwon do and arrest methods in order to help Afghan officers learn how to maintain public order.

– ROK trainers work with U.S. military police to implement a three-week training course for the Afghan National Police at Bagram Airfield. The twelve courses include instruction on police ethics, law, self-defense, marksmanship, and investigation.[17]

– KOICA was among a number of donors who contributed to the National Institution Building Project (NIBP), a United Nations Development Program (UNDP) initiative, which trained Afghan civil servants.[18]

MEDICAL AID

– Eight new ambulances were donated directly to the Parwan local government and the delivery of eight more was planned.[19]

– One hundred and thirty Afghans were sent to South Korea for medical training in 2010. Two hundred were planned for 2011.[20]

– Four health centers are to be built as a hospital within the Charikar PRT, which will work in conjunction with the Bagram Korean Hospital (BKH).

– Plans are under way for a women's health education program.[21]

EDUCATION/VOCATION

– The PRT completed in January 2012 the Korean Education and Culture Center (KECC), which hosts educational and vocational programs, such as children's education, hairdressing, literacy, sewing, and information technology (IT). Some one hundred Afghans are currently enrolled for three-month courses. Courses in the next term will be extended to five months.

– Afghan trainers are sent to South Korea for two months of training in their respective fields.

– Four district schools are to be constructed with PRT funds by 2012.

AGRICULTURAL DEVELOPMENT

- Afghan officials working in the agriculture sector are sent to South Korea for two-week training courses as part of a KOICA-UNDP project.[22]
- A model farm is planned in Charikar.
- Retaining walls were built alongside canals.[23]
- District wells were dug for local villages.[24]

THE KOREAN MEDICAL AND VOCATIONAL TRAINING TEAM

South Korea decided to establish the Korean Medical and Vocational Training Team (KMVTT) at Bagram Airfield, and in June 2008, with the Korean International Cooperation Agency taking the lead. Since February 2010, KOICA has managed the Bagram Korean Hospital (BKH) through the Inje University Paik Hospital, which runs the day-to-day operations of the hospital, provides South Korean medical staff and administrators, and trains Afghan staff and health administrators both on-site and in Korea. As of 2011, more than fifty Afghan doctors have been sent to South Korea for three-month internships. New buildings were constructed for both the hospital and training center, including a reservation center, a facility for inpatient services, and an operations room. On any given day, the BKH provides free medical care to between one hundred sixty and two hundred patients. Five South Korean doctors, four Afghan general practitioners, one dentist, and thirty-five local staff work at the hospital. Working with the Egyptian Field Hospital and U.S. base hospital, the BKH offers treatment for hypertension, cardio and neurological disorders, seizures, Parkinson's disease, and tumors. In addition, the hospital has carried out more than fifty thousand immunization shots for hepatitis B and more than five hundred thousand immunization shots for polio between 2009 and 2010.[25] Although the BKH is situated outside the Afghan medical system, it is able to make referrals to local Afghan health centers (Parwan Province has about ten comprehensive health centers) and is designed to transition eventually to Afghan administration and control.[26] BKH plays a double role as both a functioning hospital and a local anchor for Afghanistan's developing medical community. In 2009, South Korea donated one hundred new ambulances to the Afghanistan National Police, providing training to more than ninety Afghan drivers and medical staff. South Korea donated an additional eight state-of-the-art ambulances to the local district clinics in April 2011.

Despite these significant contributions, there are doubts as to whether the BKH is sustainable after transition: the level of care being provided is both high quality and high cost. Without a national healthcare system or insurance industry, it is uncertain whether Afghanistan can afford the BKH in the absence of KOICA funding. According to KOICA staff, the start-up costs for the BKH, new buildings, and equipment were $13 million. The 2011 administrative costs for the hospital were $7.4 million, and an additional $2 million went to the vocational center. The future of the BKH will depend on the ability of the Ministry of Public Health's Afghan hospital system to take on these costs, the country's obtaining more development aid, and whether KOICA is willing and able to secure funding to continue its support.

The BKH's location on a U.S. military site also raises questions as to whether the future of the hospital is linked to the future of the air base and whether it will remain part of a long-term U.S. presence in Afghanistan. Then comes the question of human know-how: medical training requires years of mentorship and internships. Transition of responsibilities to Afghan National Security Forces is expected to take place in 2014. It is unclear whether this is enough time for the current South Korean staffers to mentor their Afghan colleagues to a level where the latter are able to take over the daily operations of the hospital or whether a visiting-doctor program will be necessary.[27]

Modeled on prior South Korean experience with peacekeeping operations (PKO) missions in East Timor and Iraq, the KMVTT mission has sought to provide local economic development through basic training in core skills. According to MOFAT figures, more than $8 million was spent on establishing the KMVTT (figure as of 2007).[28] The vocational center is divided into five schools, each composed of twenty students, who undergo nine months of training in their chosen area. The five schools provide instruction on construction, electrics, welding, auto mechanics, and IT. Competition is fierce and entrants are chosen from a pool of referrals made by the provincial governor, Abdul Baseer Salangi. Finalists are selected through examination and interviews with South Korean and Afghan instructors. Many graduates go on to work for Fluor Company, an American company that carries out construction and maintenance services for Bagram Airfield, where they earn a salary more than twice as high as the average for those working outside the base.[29] All students receive basic computing courses and all work in both the metric and the English systems of measurement. Like many vocational schools, the emphasis is on practical (70 percent) on-the-shop-floor learning rather than on theory (30 percent), and many construction products of the training program are either used at the school or sold. As with the hospital, the question of sustainability of the operating costs to run the vocational center after the transition in 2014 is a critical one. At any rate, daily instruction at the school is increasingly handled by Afghans, many of whom are former students, as South Korean instructors adopt a more indirect role. This is particularly true of the construction, auto mechanic, and IT schools. There is also some concern regarding how students are chosen for the program. Some allegations have been made that local officials have used the process to shore up their political positions by nominating the sons of allies. Whatever the case, the school is run well, has a high degree of professionalism, and offers a curriculum that addresses local needs.

CHALLENGES

AN ASSESSMENT OF PARWAN PRT'S IMPACT

The contributions of provincial reconstruction teams can be determined by evaluating internal dynamics and the effect of PRTs on the community. Regarding internal dynamics, how did the South Koreans fare in addressing the challenges of interagency cooperation, and how well have they fit into local command structures of U.S., ISAF, or Afghan forces? Finally, how adept have they been at learning and applying lessons in the field?

As with most PRTs operating in Afghanistan, the South Korean mission must manage the challenge of being a hybrid civilian and military organization. This broad, integrative approach toward security and development inherent in the PRT is viewed by many as a positive, but it carries with it systematic challenges at a tactical or field level. This tension has been fairly common at the beginning of PRT operating mandates and is due primarily to the differing agency cultures, the different mandates of those agencies, and unspecified roles and responsibilities within the PRT model. Development agencies tend to be staffed by civilians with a nongovernmental organization (NGO) or private-sector background, who may find it difficult to fit into military planning and organization. Furthermore, development personnel tend to take a long view of development, striving to build institutions and capacity rather than infrastructure. This long view can sometimes contrast with that of a new PRT military commander, who is expected to make a visible, quick impact with a new bridge, new school, or some other infrastructure, which will help "win hearts and minds" and contribute to the PRT's security by improving relations between a PRT and its local community. Development agencies keen to put their efforts into building up the national government may find the majority of resources going to projects that seem focused on security rather than development objectives.

In the South Korean case, many of these problems were simplified by the fact that the PRT was run by a civilian diplomat from the Ministry of Foreign Affairs and Trade, and that the Ministry of National Defense contingent did not have any development role at all. Its main function has been to provide security for the PRT, its staff, and for South Korean development personnel operating outside the base. This has avoided tensions between the two communities over where resources should be allocated, but it did cause some initial problems in that both mission commanders—civilian and military—saw their mission objectives differently. For the South Korean military contingent, their given directive is to protect the mission and prevent casualties. The KOICA team, on the other hand, saw its mission as carrying out as many development projects as possible, given the resources and personnel available.

According to one source, the Parwan PRT was undertaking two missions a day (outside the base) under security of U.S. forces. After the handover, this dropped to four or five a month, each mission being carefully rehearsed by the ROK military contingent. However, as time has passed, the South Koreans have learned quickly—as have other nations running PRTs—that critical to the success of this divided mission profile is to incorporate lessons swiftly into operations. In addition, the civilian leader has worked closely and thoughtfully with his military counterpart to increase the number of missions while not irresponsibly endangering personnel. As with other PRT-contributing nations, South Korea has found that personal relationships between civilian and military leaders are vital to the smooth functioning of the PRT system. Furthermore, PRTs depend on the ability of different agencies and ministries to overcome their rivalries and coordinate closely back in the capital. South Korea's ability to progress in this area has been reflected in the MOFAT and MND discussions in Seoul at the end of 2010, in which MOFAT persuaded MND to undertake more missions outside the base.[30] This showed that not only were the South Koreans on the ground able to adapt quickly to the requirements of PRT interagency coordination, but also that those in the ministries back in Seoul were able to adapt to this new way of working together. One recommendation is that civilian and military leaders have joint predeployment selection and training so that the vagaries of character and personality can at least be partly shaped.

Although it is certain that the South Korean deployment of a PRT in Afghanistan has influenced perceptions of South Korea in international security operations, among local Afghan officials, U.S. officials, and other nations that deal with the South Koreans, it is still too early to determine the local population's assessment.[31] As the U.S. Embassy PRT working group in Kabul discovered, PRT assessment is extremely difficult, requiring a combination of quantitative, qualitative, and perception data.[32] Given the absence of public opinion data in Parwan province, one policy recommendation is that KOICA invest in province-wide polls to gauge Afghan response to KOICA projects. As the United Kingdom's Department for International Development (DFID) and Coffey's Helmand Monitoring and Evaluation Programme (HMEP) show, accurate data can be gathered in the most insecure environments if given adequate resources and consideration.[33]

The type of resources and time invested in the HMEP were beyond the scope of this study, but it was possible to get some idea of South Korea's influence from written and spoken interviews with U.S. and Afghan officials. Before South Korea's deployment to Afghanistan, many Afghans did not have much experience with South Korean people, culture, cuisine, or national character. The deployment has given South Korea the opportunity to expose Afghan officials to its unique development history and a development model distinct from the Western development experience. In carrying out this familiarization program, the South Korean PRT chooses a number of Parwan officials every year to go to South Korea for three-week courses on rural reconstruction and economic development. Among other things, Parwan district and provincial officials have been exposed to South Korea's remarkable industrial development, agricultural practices, and experience with rural development. This last program, known as the *Saemaeul Undong*, dates from the 1970s and stresses local community responsibility with government input, resources, and technical expertise.[34]

PERSPECTIVES ON THE ROK CONTRIBUTION

AFGHAN OFFICIALS

Interviews were carried out with Afghan government officials from the Ministry of Rural Reconstruction and Development (MRRD), the provincial governor's office, and the provincial council level. Although interviews with Afghan officials remain, for the purpose of this study, broad brushstrokes, a majority of them were positive. Many respondents stated that the PRT was excellent at consultations and tried hard to listen to Afghan needs, though the South Korean PRT has apparently favored central government over local officials. A senior official in the MRRD in Kabul, for example, was happy with South Korean cooperation with line ministry representatives. He stated how at the beginning of the deployment, the South Korean PRT director discovered that local MRRD staff lacked proper transport and immediately donated two SUVs so that MRRD could travel around the province to visit project sites. According to this individual, South Koreans met with MRRD staff regularly and tried to anticipate future needs.[35] By contrast, Afghan officials at the provincial council level and community development level stated that many major projects had already been planned and decided in Seoul before consultations. In addition, many of these were more costly than necessary: KOICA offered to build a school in Parwan for $1 million, but Afghan officials at the Ministry of Education argued that at least eight schools could be built with that funding.[36] Despite this concern, the same officials testified to the ROK PRT responsiveness to requests for short-term projects, citing the donation of computer equipment, office furniture, and the reconstruction of local government facilities.[37] The South Korean project maintenance system seems to be working in terms of interacting with local needs, contracting out to local workers, and carefully managing funding so as to avoid corruption or inefficiency. The funding method with large-scale projects is to commit 40 percent of the required funding at the start of the project, a further 40 percent after enough progress has been made, and the final 20 percent on completion of the project. There is speculation that the rocket attacks suffered by the South Korean PRT were caused by disgruntled Afghan contractors,[38] but so far no one has claimed responsibility for them, and it is just as possible that the attacks were caused by a rivalry between various militias and private security firms.[39]

U.S. OFFICIALS

U.S. officials tended to be positive about the ROK contributions at the local, provincial, and Kabul embassy levels. This stems partly from the close links between the two nations and partly from U.S. appreciation of South Korea's contribution. In the first instance, some of the U.S. officials interviewed had actually served in South Korea or had previously dealt with the South Korean military. Two sources noted the South Korean military's professionalism, in addition to its growing expeditionary capability, which had clearly progressed since 2004, when South Korea deployed forces to Iraq.[40] One U.S. military official acknowledged that South Korean forces were highly restricted in their ability to operate. However, he sympathized with the South Korean military and felt that this restriction stemmed from South Korean domestic political sensitivities, and that it was gradually evolving toward a situation in which South Korea might contribute more forces to international security operations. Still, due to security restrictions, South Korea carries out projects in only five of Parwan's ten districts, with the United States covering the other areas. This arrangement is actually typical in Afghanistan. In all cases, U.S. officials expressed gratitude for the ROK's sizable contribution, in both personnel and resources, to the Afghanistan mission.

INTERNATIONAL AND NONGOVERNMENTAL ORGANIZATION OFFICIALS

For the purpose of this study, the author met with a number of international governmental organization (IGO) and NGO officials who carry out development work within the Parwan area. Their perception was that the South Korean PRT suffered from civil-military problems

initially, but that it has improved with time and experience. They attrib-
uted difficulties to a lack of South Korean experience in complex operations before Afghanistan and Iraq, as well as to the complex bureaucratic
structures necessitated by the ROK's comprehensive approach. One
IGO official noted that much South Korean project work was carried
out without proper consultation with the United Nations Assistance
Mission to Afghanistan (UNAMA), but also stated that this was true
of U.S. as well as other allies' operations, giving the impression that
this complaint was generic rather than specific to South Korea's PRT.
Another complaint is that the long-term project schedule of the PRT
was too slow and that too few projects were in the pipeline; however,
this was probably due to security and contractor issues, as much as to
South Korean inexperience. UNAMA officials reinforced the impression that the South Korean PRT preferred to consult with line ministries linked to Kabul rather than to their local Parwan counterparts and
that many development projects in the pipeline had not been carried out
with enough local discussion. As with Afghan officials, the UNAMA
team said that South Korea's approach to development was still slightly
askew with local conditions in Afghanistan, in that costs were too high
for the Afghan context and that much of the planning and decision-
making was being done in Seoul rather than locally.

CONCLUSION

The deployment of the South Korean PRT to Afghanistan is a water-
shed in South Korean military and development history. The event
is remarkable in different ways: first, it is another milestone in South
Korea's arrival as a global provider—rather than just a beneficiary—of
security; second, the scale of the commitment in terms of personnel and
financial contributions testifies to the ability and willingness of South
Korea to operate in areas where its national interests are more widely
defined, including geographically beyond the Korean peninsula. South
Korean individuals interviewed consistently stated that it was time for
South Korea "to give back to the international community" and cited
the United Nations' involvement in the Korean War as part of the legacy
of obligation. The PRT deployment is remarkable, because it testifies to
South Korea's growing expeditionary capabilities. It is an example of
the MND's ability to deploy a large contingent and manage the logistics,

planning, and communications for the unit, which reveals a growing sophistication in the MND's capabilities. That this particular operation has been a joint one is a further achievement, in indicating that the MND is able to smoothly fit into the Regional Command East structure and to operate under multinational command. Finally, this deployment of the Charikar PRT is remarkable because it is the first time that an East Asian nation has worked with a civil-military structure. It has experienced some of the same interministerial tensions as other PRTs, and it will be interesting to see what coordination mechanism develops to deal with these problems. In the United Kingdom, this problem led to the creation of a coordinating agency, the Post-Conflict Reconstruction Unit (PCRU), now called the Stabilization Unit, which borrows personnel from DFID, the Foreign and Commonwealth Office, and the Ministry of Defense in an effort to get "jointness." The United States developed the Office of the Coordinator for Reconstruction and Stabilization (S/CRS) within the Department of State for a similar function. How will South Korea deal with these issues? Perhaps the answer will be uniquely South Korean.

MOVING FORWARD

As the United States enters into a new and difficult time of budgetary austerity, the cutting of excess expenditure is offset by a shift of diplomatic and military resources to the Asia Pacific. China's decades-long rise, the translation of its economic prowess into new military capabilities, and the nervousness it has engendered in the region have impelled the United States to reassure its allies while also seeking their greater participation in maintaining the security order. This reading is supported, in the short term, by Secretary of State Hillary Clinton's article "America's Pacific Century" and Secretary of Defense Leon Panetta's visit to the region in October 2011.[41] Long-term support for this argument can be seen in the United States' sustained diplomatic reinvigoration of alliances and quasi-alliances. The United States' close collaboration with allies like South Korea in expeditionary capabilities and in complex operations not only helps the United States maintain its commitments abroad, but also encourages South Korea to contribute to security. These benefits brought to Washington by South Korean inclusion in its campaign in Afghanistan are mirrored by the benefits brought to Seoul by its participation. It strengthens and boosts

U.S.-ROK interoperability and planning abroad, and it develops skill sets among South Korea's ministries that might prove vital in any contingency involving North Korean collapse.

The final analysis of the South Korean PRT at Charikar has been that it is in many ways a model of South Korea itself: hierarchical and civilian led; disciplined and passionate about its goals. South Korea's desire to become a provider of security pushes it beyond its comfort zone in some ways, but in other ways, this is precisely what is needed for growth. The development of East Asia as the global driver for economic growth has meant that East Asian culture and methodologies are increasingly under scrutiny in the West and non-Western world. While South Korea is currently working closely with the United States to understand how U.S. PRTs behave in Afghanistan, its answers are not American answers. Its development model, its unique history, and its culture give these problems a different twist that U.S. military and development policymakers might do well to study.

Counterproliferation and South Korea: From Local to Global

Scott Bruce

The Republic of Korea's (ROK) participation in and adherence to global nonproliferation norms has been driven by its relationship with the United States and the North Korean nuclear issue. South Korea's role in international counterproliferation and interdiction efforts, such as the Proliferation Security Initiative (PSI), has been based on a need to support its alliance with the United States and a desire to block, where possible, the exports of nuclear and conventional weapons technology by North Korea. The ROK has established itself as a champion of multilateral export control regimes by adopting a sophisticated export control system while remaining an export-oriented business and shipping hub for high-tech goods in northeast Asia. The improvement in these export control systems, however, was made under pressure from the U.S. government to catch up to the security concerns created by ROK high-tech exports.

The extent to which these contributions to counterproliferation are global is thus debatable. The North Korean nuclear program is a global threat to nonproliferation norms, but it is a local threat to South Korea. The ROK's concern over the Democratic People's Republic of Korea's (DPRK) nuclear ambitions is based on the direct security threat it poses to the South, rather than on the damage the North's nuclear breakout has done to the Nuclear Nonproliferation Treaty. The role of the U.S.-ROK security alliance, developed in the Korean War, strengthened throughout the Cold War, and maintained after the collapse of the Soviet Union to counter the North Korean nuclear and conventional threat to the South, is a unique relationship. The extent to which the ROK has shifted policy based on influence from the United States, then, is arguably not an example of global leadership, but instead a need to address the concerns of a great power with a shared security interest.

Although the ROK is a positive example of adherence to counterproliferation regimes and sets a global example of coordinating economic growth with contribution to such efforts, the true global dimension of the ROK's contribution to counterproliferation efforts is best demonstrated in policy issues that are not related to the North Korean nuclear program and independent of the U.S.-ROK relationship. One potential area for South Korea to demonstrate this global contribution is as an emerging nuclear power vendor. South Korea should use its role as an exporter of nuclear energy technology to make a truly global contribution to nonproliferation norms, such as securing nuclear material, encouraging adherence to international nonproliferation regimes, and marketing proliferation-resistant nuclear power systems that support the increasing global interest in nuclear power while minimizing the risk of nuclear proliferation.

INTERDICTION AND THE PROLIFERATION SECURITY INITIATIVE

The Proliferation Security Initiative is an interesting case for evaluating the ROK's global role in counterproliferation, because South Korea's evolution from an observer of PSI drills to becoming part of the strategic planning team for the initiative was directly related to the North Korean nuclear program and pressure from the United States. South Korea's contribution to this global counterproliferation effort stemmed from a local need to support U.S.-sponsored, multilateral efforts at counterproliferation and to respond to North Korea's second nuclear test.

In November 2002, Spanish authorities, acting on a request from the United States, interdicted the *So San*, a Cambodian vessel shipping Scud missiles, explosive warheads, rocket fuel, and other unidentified chemicals from the DPRK to Yemen. The *So San* case raised a problem for counterproliferation efforts in that suspicion of transport of weapons of mass destruction (WMD) is not grounds for search and seizure of a vessel under the United Nations Convention on the Law of the Sea (UNCLOS). Consequently, in 2003 the Bush administration launched PSI. A nonbinding commitment from participating states to interdict transfers of nuclear and other WMD, PSI is an "activity, not an organization."[1] Countries that endorse the principles of PSI pledge to carry out interdictions under existing export law, using what has been called a broken-taillight scenario to interdict any suspicious cargo using established legal means.

South Korea's role in PSI has changed along with the development of the DPRK nuclear program and ROK relations with Washington. South Korea was ambivalent toward the initiative during the Roh Moo-hyun administration and declined to endorse PSI's principles on the basis of concerns that such a move would harm inter-Korea relations and that the interdiction of a North Korean vessel by an ROK ship could lead to conflict.[2] However, in response to pressure from the United States and other countries to participate, it did agree to become an observer of PSI drills.[3]

Although concerns over PSI prevailed under the Roh government, they were far from unanimous within the administration. The Ministry of Foreign Affairs and Trade considered ROK participation in PSI "inevitable," which caused significant alarm within the progressive administration.[4] Ministry staff would later recommend to the Lee Myung-bak transition team that the initiative "be given serious consideration."[5] The prevailing assessment of PSI under the Roh government was that the risk of conflict with the North was greater than the benefits of adopting its principles.

The Lee Myung-bak administration had a different attitude toward PSI. Although the transition team was clear that there would be no immediate endorsements of its principles, members of the Lee cabinet expressed interest in joining the initiative early in the new government's tenure.[6] The ROK announced it would review its stance on the initiative after the April 2009 North Korean long-range missile test and adopted the initiative's principles on May 26, 2009, two days after the second North Korean nuclear test. ROK foreign minister Yu Myun-hwan made the relationship between the DPRK nuclear program and the decision to join PSI explicit, noting that "Our participation in the [Proliferation Security Initiative] is necessary, in light of the very grave situation that North Korea has conducted a nuclear test."[7] The Lee administration, more aligned with the United States and dealing with a North that had cut off communications with the South, saw little reason not to join the initiative.

Since adopting the principles of PSI, South Korea has become highly active in its work. In October 2010, the ROK hosted Exercise Eastern Endeavor, a maritime PSI drill that practiced the interdiction of ships suspected of carrying weapons of mass destruction.[8] Later that month, South Korea hosted a regional workshop for PSI in Busan, and in November joined the PSI Operation Experts Group (OEG), which oversees the policy and operations of PSI.[9] The ROK government stated that its role in OEG will strengthen its ability to "monitor illegal weapons trade and related activities in North Korea."[10]

The ability to assess the effectiveness of PSI, let alone the ROK's contribution to it, is challenging. First, given that PSI is a rigid enforcement of existing export control laws, it is difficult to determine whether these interdictions would have happened had PSI not been developed. It is possible, particularly after the passage of UN Security Council Resolution 1874, which calls on all UN states to inspect North Korean cargo that comes through their country, that many of these interdictions would have occurred without PSI.

Second, one of the benefits of the initiative is its deterrent aspect. The multistate exercises, which often featured speeches by leading officials, were meant to send a message to North Korea and other states that their neighbors were working together to restrict trade in WMD.[11] PSI participants in northeast Asia, each with strong navies and disputed territorial boundaries, are well acquainted with interdiction and interception of vessels, making the value of the exercises more symbolic than operationally necessary. A recent study by Joshua Pollack of North Korean missile sales shows "no meaningful change in the pattern of missile deliveries after the introduction of PSI."[12] It is thus difficult to assess what impact this deterrent aspect of PSI has had on shipment of WMD and how much the ROK has contributed to it.

Finally, government statements are inconsistent in their assessment of the success of PSI. In 2006, the United States credited PSI with interdicting more than thirty shipments of WMD or related material, including the interdiction of centrifuges that played a significant role in convincing Libya to end its nuclear and chemical weapons program.[13] In practice, any successful interdiction during the Bush administration was counted as a win for PSI. The Obama administration, though it has continued to participate in the initiative and has pledged to turn it into a "durable international effort," has also downplayed its role in interdictions and deemphasized PSI as part of its counterproliferation efforts.[14] These factors make it difficult to assess the success of PSI, let alone the ROK's contribution to its efforts.

In several cases, PSI, in conjunction with UN Security Council Resolution 1874, appears to have played a significant role. The search of a North Korean shipping container in Busan in September 2009, which found clothing that could be used in the manufacture of chemical weapons, was credited to PSI.[15] There is also a relationship between PSI and the interdiction of the *M/V Light* in June 2011. The ship was falsely flying a flag of Belize, a member of PSI, which gave the United States permission to inspect the ship. After ignoring U.S. attempts to hail the vessel and refusing requests to board the ship, the *M/V Light* reversed course and turned back toward North Korea.[16] Since Belize gave the United States permission to inspect the ship and the *M/V Light* refused, the ship was then technically stateless, allowing the United States to board it freely. The relationship with Belize under PSI was cited as an important factor in forcing the vessel to return to port.

In other cases, the relationship between the interdiction of a North Korean vessel or shipment and PSI is more opaque. Thai authorities impounded a shipment of thirty-five tons of weapons, including missile parts, reportedly bound for Iran from North Korea in December 2009.[17] Thailand has not endorsed PSI, so it is hard to relate this interdiction to the initiative. South Africa, also not a PSI member state, intercepted a shipment bound for the Republic of the Congo carrying North Korean tank parts in February 2010.[18] The *Kung Nam I*, a North Korean vessel believed to be carrying a shipment of weapons to Myanmar in June 2009, returned to port in the DPRK.[19] The ship was not intercepted, making the role of PSI unclear, but many have suggested that the visibility from the coordinated tracking of the ship put pressure on countries to deny harbor to the ship.

Additionally, it is worth noting that, although South Korea has joined PSI, it has never performed a maritime interdiction of a North Korean vessel under the initiative. Such an action would mean a confrontation between ROK and DPRK vessels—one that could easily escalate into a wider conflict that would violate the Armistice Agreement.[20] A clash is certainly imaginable after the *Cheonan* incident, and South Korea has so far let the U.S. Navy take the lead in hailing suspicious North Korean vessels. This might be interpreted as a credibility gap when it comes to ROK participation in the initiative.

Although it is difficult to assess the contribution South Korea has made to global counterproliferation efforts under the PSI, a few things can be said about South Korea's role in the initiative. First, South Korea has moved from ambivalence toward PSI to playing a leading role in this effort—hosting a PSI exercise and a workshop and overseeing policy and operations. Second, the changes in South Korea's status with regard to PSI were driven both by North Korean belligerence and by pressure from the United States. The ROK joined PSI in response to the 2009

DPRK missile and nuclear tests and hosted its first exercise under PSI shortly after the sinking of the *Cheonan*. Third, although there may be activities that have not been made public, particularly given the Obama administration's downplaying the initiative in its counterproliferation strategy, PSI activities that have been publicized have been focused on North Korea. Stemming the flow of WMD from North Korea to other states in the region has a global effect, but North Korea is a local problem for South Korea. Restricting North Korea's WMD exports is a bigger domestic priority for South Korea than restricting proliferation outside of northeast Asia. Although South Korea is playing a global role in counterproliferation efforts through the PSI, it is being driven by local concerns unique to the ROK.

ROK CAPABILITIES AND THE POTENTIAL TO ENHANCE THE ROLE OF THE PSI

The ROK's role as a networked, middle power with positive relations with most states in the region gives it a unique capability to support and potentially expand the role of PSI. South Korea plays an important role as a moderator among the great powers of the region. Although it has a strong tie to the United States through the ROK-U.S. security alliance, South Korea also has positive trade relations with China, has remained carefully neutral in the South China Sea conflict, and has not established itself as a competitor with the Chinese on security issues, as the Japanese have.[21]

The People's Republic of China remains a gaping hole in PSI. The North Korean tank parts intercepted in South Africa were shipped from China, and the small-arms and missile parts bound to Iran from North Korea used Chinese airspace for two-thirds of its trip.[22] China has not endorsed the principles of PSI and considers it an extension of the U.S. hard-line policy toward North Korea. While it is highly unlikely that China will change its position on PSI, South Korea could play a role in narrowing the gap between the Chinese and U.S. perspectives. This would give China an opportunity to earn some credibility as a positive actor when it comes to counterproliferation efforts and allow South Korea to act as a mediator between the United States and China in a way that will expand South Korea's networked role in northeast Asia.[23]

South Korea can also use its balancing role to promote PSI and related counterproliferation efforts in other states in the region. Of the

Association of Southeast Asian Nations (ASEAN) states, only Brunei, Cambodia, Singapore, and the Philippines are members of PSI. South Korea can act as an emissary for PSI to these countries by promoting the use of PSI in conjunction with UN Security Council Resolution 1874. The resolution adds increased legitimacy to PSI's efforts by making the interdiction of suspicious North Korean vessels a mandatory activity for all UN member states. This might dissuade states from offering North Korean vessels innocent passage through their territorial waters or allowing them to refuel at their ports.[24] Although Thailand is not a PSI member, it has shown that it is willing to comply with the UNSC resolution to interdict shipments from North Korea.

As a state with obvious concerns over the North Korean nuclear program, South Korea can also work with PSI member states in the region to provide advance consent for other PSI states to board suspicious vessels that may be falsely flying their flag.[25] For states that have not joined PSI, South Korea can promote cooperation with PSI member states, if not achieve wholesale endorsement of PSI's principles.

Another opportunity to expand PSI would be to focus on small ships. Bruce Bechtol argues that, given a lack of other viable delivery options, the North Koreans could place a nuclear weapon in a small merchant vessel or trawler and sail it into a South Korean or Japanese port.[26] This is one of the only real offensive deployments of a North Korean nuclear weapon possible.[27] Small vessels are also a danger for shipping nuclear technology and other WMD-related materials.[28] PSI has, so far, focused mostly on tracking large vessels. South Korea, with the most experience in detecting and intercepting small North Korean vessels and with increased sensitivity toward any North Korean ships after the *Cheonan* incident, could take a leading role in expanding PSI to focus more on small ships.[29]

SOUTH KOREA AND MULTILATERAL EXPORT CONTROL REGIMES

ESTABLISHING A ROBUST SET OF EXPORT CONTROLS

South Korea has demonstrated that it can offset the need to monitor and control exports to prevent the spread of nuclear technology and maintain a high-tech economy. However, this process came about from pressure from the United States to reform the South Korean system. Even though the ROK is now an exemplar of a high-tech, export-oriented economy that has adopted comprehensive and efficient export controls, the ROK's global contribution to counterproliferation in this area is not clear.

South Korea is a high-tech economy that specializes in the manufacture of semiconductors, communications technology, computers, and chemicals and has an advanced nuclear power technology program, all of which have dual-use components. Furthermore, the ROK is a major transit and transshipment hub in northeast Asia. This means that South Korea must delicately coordinate the demands of its export-based economy with the need to control sensitive materials and address proliferation concerns.

Over the past decade, the ROK's export control system has evolved from a loose system with minimal penalties for export violations to an advanced system for tracking exports, with serious consequences for noncompliance. This transformation was driven by pressure from the United States, which repeatedly threatened to sanction South Korean firms unless the ROK took measures to control its exports of sensitive technology.[30]

Although the ROK joined the Nuclear Suppliers Group (NSG) in 1995, the Australia Group in 1996, and the Wassenaar Arrangement on Export Controls for Conventional Arms and Dual-Use Goods and Technologies in 1996, the agreements have not been adequately enforced.[31] For example, Hanbando Balance Inc. shipped balancing machines to Libya that could be used in the construction of centrifuges.[32] Although the balancing machines were controlled under ROK law, the goods were exported without a license.[33] In another case, a South Korean firm sold sodium cyanide to North Korea via China without a license.[34] Although the legislation was in place, exporters did not understand it and were not complying with the regulations.

South Korea slowly made the legislative and institutional changes required to stem export control violations. In December 2002, South Korea issued the Public Notice on Exports and Imports of Strategic Items and adopted a catch-all export control system in January 2003, which added restrictions to sensitive, but not restricted, items based on the end user.[35] South Korea also adopted its Strategic-Item Export Control Information System in 2005, which allowed companies to apply for permission to export goods online and a coding system that allowed exporters to check if their goods were restricted.[36]

These changes were in part driven by a high-profile failure of the ROK export control system. Kyongdo Enterprises, a South Korean company, was found to have shipped nickel and tritium to Iran in 2004 and 2005.[37] These materials can be used to construct triggers for nuclear weapons and are tightly controlled. The materials were shipped from Moscow to Incheon and then on to Iran, but the ROK had no legislation in place to impose export controls on goods transshipped through the ROK, even if shipped by South Korean firms. This incident made the inadequacies of the ROK export control system clear and increased pressure on the Ministry of Commerce, Industry, and Energy to reform.[38]

A critical issue in reforming export controls in the ROK was public understanding of the system. As recently as 2005, a poll by the Korea International Trade Association found that, though most Koreans supported the idea of export controls, two-thirds of export companies did not understand the export control system.[39] Eleven percent had "never heard of the export control system" at all.[40] Less than 40 percent of these firms regularly secured authorization from the government before they exported materials abroad or checked to see whether their exports were prohibited.[41]

It was strange to many South Koreans that the government went from trying to promote exports to controlling them. A major institution in informing the public was the Strategic Trade Information Center (STIC), later the Korea Strategic Trade Institute (KOSTI), which offered formal training in export controls.[42] Although STIC was initially small, with only eight staff members overseeing a country with annual exports in excess of $250 billion, the ROK government expanded the staff rapidly.[43] STIC focused enforcement on large companies, such as Samsung Electronics and Hynix Semiconductor, and then attempted to encourage cooperation between large and small companies to spread the knowledge of the system.[44]

Given the limited understanding of export control laws in the ROK, South Korean authorities generally accepted pleas of innocent negligence and offered amnesty to those caught in violation of the law. The head of a South Korean firm that exported sodium cyanide to North Korea was given a suspended sentence.[45] Two other cases, one involving the planned export of air compressor machines, which could be used to make missile warheads, and another involving material that could be used for enriching uranium, were dismissed with no consequences after the companies committed to stricter adherence to export control laws in the future.[46] In one case, the owner of an ROK company claimed innocent negligence and was released without punishment for shipping potassium bifluoride, but he was arrested again six months later for attempting the same shipment to the same destination.[47]

Even when the exports were clearly intentional, punishment was still light. In 2006 and 2007, Lee Tae-young, former president of the Daewoo Group, illegally sent military equipment to Myanmar in exchange for the rights to develop a natural gas project there. The export was intentional, and the company was well acquainted with ROK export control law, but Lee was fined only $50,000 and given a one-year suspended sentence.[48] Still, in general, enforcement has been stepped up and penalties have been strengthened.[49]

South Korea has also adopted legislation to control transshipments within its boundaries. In 2012, ROK authorities identified an attempt to export luxury cars from Japan to the DPRK via South Korea. This was the first known scheme to use South Korea as an en route destination for the illegal shipment of goods to North Korea. The identification of the cargo shows an increased ability of the ROK to monitor transshipments.[50] However, in terms of preventing the flow of goods to North Korea, the increased ability of the ROK to monitor the shipment of goods most likely means that most of these items will be transported through China or another country.

In terms of institutions, although the ROK government has increased its oversight of different areas and streamlined the approval process, different ministries with overlapping roles are still involved in the export process. The Ministry of Knowledge Economy (MKE) sets the standards for dual-use and catch-alls; the Ministry of Science, Education, and Technology (MEST) controls nuclear items that may be prohibited under the nuclear suppliers group; and the Defense Acquisition Program Administration (DAPA) controls exports and imports related to the defense industry. The exception to all of these is the Ministry of Unification (MOU), which manages the export or import of any of these items to North Korea. The MOU, however, may lack the technical skills to determine the suitability of an item and may have to liaise with the MKE to make a determination. The interactions of these bureaucracies, each with their own watch lists and item controls, can be challenging. For example, a company wanting to export a product related to military technology would first have to obtain a recommendation from DAPA before submitting a request for an export license to MEST, which might have to work with MOFAT on the issue.[51] If software came with the technology, then the license would also be controlled under the Australia Declaration and therefore would involve the MKE.[52] Figure 6 lists controlled items and the ROK agencies responsible for licensing and classification.

Although South Korea has transitioned from a country with a porous export control system to one with a strong set of controls, it has yet to establish a global role for itself. It is a powerful example of how to reconcile the needs of an export-oriented economy with the need to control sensitive technology. South Korea also understands the legal and institutional measures needed to adopt and enforce comprehensive controls. That said, while it is in full compliance with international standards, it has not yet begun to work with other states to bring them into line with those standards.

FIGURE 6. CONTROLLED ITEMS AND AGENCIES RESPONSIBLE FOR LICENSING AND CLASSIFICATION

Items		Export License Agency	Classification Agency
Strategic Items	Dual-use Items	Export Control Policy Division, Ministry of Knowledge Economy	Korea Strategic Trade Institute (KOSTI)
	NSG Trigger Items	Nuclear Control Team, Ministry of Education, Science, and Technology	Korea Institute of Nuclear Nonproliferation and Control
	Munitions	Export Cooperation Division, Defense Acquisition Program Administration	Export Cooperation Division, Defense Acquisition Program Administration
Catch-alls	Nonstrategic Items	Export Control Policy Division, Ministry of Knowledge Economy	
Notes	1. Direct export/import of the above items to and from North Korea is managed by Ministry of Unification based on the Inter-Korea Exchange and Cooperation Act		
	2. Customs clearance run by the clearance planning division of the Korea Customs Service, under the Customs Act		

Source: Yes Trade, http://www.yestrade.go.kr/portl/html/eng/sub02/s02_2.jsp.

THE ROLE OF U.S.-ROK RELATIONS AND OPPORTUNITIES TO ENHANCE KOREA'S GLOBAL ROLE

The U.S. and ROK relationship was decisive in moving South Korea from a state with little interest in implementing trade controls to a champion of export controls.[53] U.S. pressure was influential in encouraging South Korea to implement and enforce real controls. It has also been important in encouraging the ROK to contribute to sanctions against Iran, which supplies the ROK with around 10 percent of its energy, and to bring the ROK into the Missile Technology Control Regime (MTCR).[54] U.S. missile assistance allowed the ROK to support the MTCR but retain access to missile technology it needed to defend against the DPRK. On the same day that the ROK joined the MTCR, it negotiated an agreement with Washington to extend its maximum missile range.[55] As the ROK foreign ministry statement noted when it joined the MTCR, "by adopting the new guideline, our government will be able to develop and possess missiles with enough range capabilities to meet our security needs."[56]

Countries without strong export controls require funding and training to implement a comprehensive and effective system. Having made these changes in the recent past and having good relations with its neighbors in East Asia, South Korea can provide training programs on export controls to other states in the region. The ROK can work through ASEAN or the ASEAN Regional Forum to instruct other countries about what technologies require restrictions, implement new legislation, and reorganize government institutions for strategic trade controls, and it can encourage these states to participate in multilateral export control regimes.

Another potential area for the ROK to have a global impact on export controls is to work on compliance for UNSC resolutions 1540 and 1373. These resolutions, which require all UN member states to take measures to prevent nuclear material and technology from falling into the hands of terrorists, involve both legal and technical compliance issues. It is a challenge for states with limited understanding of WMD programs and limited domestic legislation controlling trade on items that could be used in the manufacture of WMD to legislate and organize agencies for compliance with the laws.[57] Furthermore, in Southeast Asia in particular, states are wary of legalistic, international legislation that is not compatible with local, informal legal cultures.[58] With the exception of the Philippines, Singapore, Vietnam, and Indonesia, no other ASEAN states have responded to the 1540 committee's requests for additional information on 1540 implementation and compliance.[59] The ROK is in good standing in its implementation of the measure and can play a regional or global role in helping other states come into full compliance with the resolution.

Japan, the United States, and Australia have each made efforts to start bilateral assistance to encourage 1540 compliance.[60] South Korea, which lacks some of the historical baggage that those countries have in the region, could support these training programs to increase their effectiveness by coordinating among the trainers.[61] This work could also involve the ASEAN Regional Forum, which has had discussions on 1540 compliance.[62] Such activity would be an opportunity for South Korea to go from being a champion of export control law to setting a global standard for counterproliferation.

NUCLEAR SECURITY

DEVELOPING AN ADVANCED NUCLEAR POWER INDUSTRY

South Korea has an advanced nuclear power industry and is emerging as an exporter of nuclear technology. Although the ROK's access to nuclear technology is limited by the U.S.-South Korea Atomic Energy Agreement and the 1992 Joint Declaration on the Denuclearization of the Korean Peninsula, the export of nuclear technology allows the ROK to emerge as a global leader in nuclear nonproliferation.

The planning and construction of the ROK's first nuclear power plant began in 1957, and its first reactor was turned on in 1962.[63] Today, the ROK has developed generation III+ nuclear reactions, such as the APR-1400.[64] The twenty-one nuclear reactors in Korea provide approximately 30 percent of the ROK's generated energy, and nineteen more plants are planned to come online before 2030 to raise that total to 59 percent.[65]

As befitting an advanced nuclear power, South Korea is a contributor to several international nuclear security institutions. The ROK's international input into nuclear security issues often focuses more on North Korea than on other issues. The ROK is part of the Global Initiative to Combat Nuclear Terrorism (GICNT), which is aimed at securing fissile material and keeping nuclear material out of the hands of terrorists.[66] In June 2011, the ROK hosted the GICNT plenary meeting, which included participants from eighty-six nations.[67] Despite having an agenda focused on nuclear terrorism, the South Korean statement at the meeting focused on North Korea:

> The international community must show North Korea that it is facing a unified and resolute front, urging it to abandon all nuclear programs, including the UEP (uranium enrichment program), and cease all related activities in full compliance with U.N. Security Council resolutions 1718 and 1874.[68]

South Korea also hosts the annual ROK-UN Joint Conference on Disarmament and Nonproliferation, also known as the Jeju Process, with the UN Office of Disarmament Affairs. The conference "brings together government officials, academics, independent experts, and civil society representatives" to discuss nonproliferation issues on both the "global and regional levels."[69] The December 2010 workshop focused on managing the global spread of nuclear power with the need for nuclear security.[70] Yet the opening and closing statements by Cho Hyun, the deputy minister for multilateral, global, and legal affairs at the Ministry of Foreign Affairs and Trade, also called for action against North Korea in the wake of the November shelling of Yeongpyeong Island, showing the persistence of the DPRK issue in the ROK's counterproliferation efforts.[71]

EXPORT OF NUCLEAR TECHNOLOGY

While South Korea has been promoting regional and global nuclear nonproliferation efforts, it has also been emerging as an exporter of nuclear technology. Current plans call for the export of eighty nuclear power plants by 2030.[72] In December 2009, the ROK reached an agreement with the United Arab Emirates (UAE) to construct four 1,400-megawatt reactors.[73] South Korea has signed an agreement to build a 5-megawatt research reactor in Jordan.[74] In the future, other possible agreements in the Middle East include Saudi Arabia and Egypt.[75] The ROK signed a nuclear cooperation deal with India in July 2011.[76] South Korea has also developed footholds in Latin America and Africa by signing agreements or memoranda of understanding to cooperate on nuclear power plants and technology with Argentina and South Africa.[77] The ROK is laying the groundwork for nuclear work in Southeast Asia via discussions on possible nuclear plants in Indonesia, Thailand, Malaysia, and Singapore.[78] The deal with Indonesia is contentious due to local concerns over the plant's siting on an active seismic zone and the fatwa that the local population has declared against nuclear power.[79]

The ROK has competed on several other nuclear contracts with mixed success. Korea Electric Power Corporation failed to win contracts in Vietnam, Turkey, and Lithuania.[80] South Korea has strong business relations in the UAE through the development of an oil field and other infrastructure projects financed by South Korea, but such relationships were not present in Turkey and the parties could not agree on a price.[81]

To limit the risk that these nuclear exports will lead to a nuclear breakout, Seoul has supported the U.S. Department of Energy's Next Generation Safeguards Initiative, which looks to develop nuclear technology with built-in "safeguards by design."[82] South Korea has also proposed human resource development to identify and train nuclear engineers to develop these safeguards.[83]

The MKE has revised the ROK's export controls related to nuclear materials, added a new database to track all shipments of nuclear materials and technology overseas, and started the International Nuclear Graduate School in 2010 to train nuclear engineers in countries planning or considering the use of nuclear power.[84] The ROK is promoting the use of nuclear energy, with itself as a seller of the technology, in ASEAN and through an International Atomic Energy Agency (IAEA) program in which the ROK will share information about nuclear safety to interested countries.[85]

The Fukushima nuclear disaster has not disrupted South Korea's plans to export nuclear reactor technology. ROK president Lee Myung-bak called the use of nuclear energy "inevitable" even after the disaster, and called for transparency to address concerns about its use, touting Korean reactors as "unrivaled" in safety.[86] While Japan, despite a pledge to continue with nuclear exports, has demonstrated some ambivalence over the continued use of nuclear power, South Korea has doubled down on nuclear exports post-Fukushima.[87]

ESTABLISHING A GLOBAL NONPROLIFERATION ROLE

As a nuclear technology exporter, Seoul has an opportunity to establish nuclear standards that can support nonproliferation efforts globally. Having experimented with its own nuclear weapons program in the

1970s, South Korea is familiar with the ways that a country could attempt to obfuscate a nuclear program. In the ROK's experience, the nuclear gambit under Park Chung-hee gave South Korea neither a nuclear weapon nor access to significant new technology, and it left the ROK less secure by weakening the U.S.-ROK security alliance.[88] This gives Seoul a unique perspective on nuclear development in North Korea.

Additionally, one of the lessons of the Fukushima disaster is that building a nuclear weapon requires significant resources and carries high risk, but an attack on a nuclear facility or spent-fuel storage site can produce a nuclear explosion at a reduced cost. This threat is new to many states, but military planners in Seoul have long understood the vulnerability of the ROK's nuclear power plants from attack by the DPRK. In fact, one of the competitive features of the ROK plants is their increased shielding against missile attacks.[89] Creating standards for the physical safety of nuclear facilities from attack is an issue to which South Korea can and should make a unique contribution.

The ROK should ensure that its emergence as a nuclear technology exporter helps establish global nonproliferation norms. First, the ROK should require adoption of the IAEA Additional Protocol for all states to which it supplies nuclear technology. So far South Korea, not wanting to lose potential markets for its nuclear technology, has said that it would do so only if required by the Nuclear Suppliers Group.[90] Japan, by contrast, has made ratification of the additional protocol a condition for the transfer of nuclear technology. Therefore, Japan is not able to compete for nuclear contracts in places like Egypt and Argentina.[91] Second, South Korea should work with the NSG to restrict the transfer of enrichment and reprocessing technology—although this would likely close the door on the export of nuclear technology to India. In both of these cases, Seoul has an opportunity to advance nuclear security and nonproliferation norms as it advances as a global exporter of nuclear technology.

SOUTH KOREA'S CONTRIBUTION TO COUNTERPROLIFERATION

South Korea has made significant contributions to nonproliferation. It has vehemently opposed the North Korean nuclear program and its global proliferation threat, supporting both negotiations with the DPRK over its nuclear program and pressure, including sanctions, on the North to restrict its nuclear trade. These efforts have implications on the Korean peninsula, in northeast Asia, and globally as they attempt to halt the DPRK's established trade in weapons of mass destruction and the weakening of global nonproliferation norms that comes with the North's nuclear breakout.

Although these efforts have had a global consequence, they have in many ways been local efforts. South Korea's work on interdiction via PSI, its role in multilateral forums such as GICNT, and other measures stems from a response to a domestic security threat from North Korea. This is not to say that because South Korea has a strong self-interest in addressing the North Korean nuclear threat that its contribution does not matter. Rather, South Korea's response to the nuclear threat it faces is globally significant, but has established neither a standard that can be applied elsewhere nor a new means of addressing it. Likewise, although South Korea is a model participant in counterproliferation and nuclear security efforts, which have had a global impact by supporting the interdiction of ships carrying WMD, restricting trade in sensitive technologies, and supporting multilateral and international nonproliferation efforts, it has not established a new mechanism for addressing these issues nor has it been active in transferring its success to other states.

What then should South Korea do to contribute to international nonproliferation? It should establish an ROK model for building a legal and institutional infrastructure needed to control sensitive technology while maintaining a strong, export-oriented economy. This model should include increased collaboration on interdiction, not only involving North Korea, but also focusing on other states—in particular, the role of networked middle powers like the ROK. It could also entail South Korea's moving beyond participation in multilateral and global nonproliferation efforts to start setting the agenda for future initiatives on nuclear security. Finally, it should involve promoting nuclear security by establishing standards for the export of nuclear power that require participation in important international nonproliferation agreements, as well as standards for the use of technology that is safer from accident or attack and minimizes the risk of a nuclear breakout.

Endnotes

OVERVIEW

1. Stockholm International Peace Research Institute (SIPRI) Yearbook Online, "The 15 countries with the highest military expenditure in 2010," http://www.sipriyearbook. org/view/9780199695522/sipri-9780199695522-div1-44.xml.
2. Ministry of National Defense of the Republic of Korea, *Defense White Paper,* 2010, http://www.mnd.go.kr/cms_file/info/mndpaper/2010/2010WhitePaperAll_eng.pdf.
3. Lee Myung-bak, "Together We Shall Open a Road to Advancement," speech delivered at President Lee Myung-bak's inaugural ceremony, February 25, 2008, http://english. hani.co.kr/arti/english_edition/e_national/271850.html.
4. Korea International Cooperation Agency (KOICA), "Annual Report 2010," http:// www.koica.go.kr/upload/pr/annual/2010annual_e.pdf.
5. The White House, Office of the Press Secretary, "Joint Vision for the Alliance of the United States of America and the Republic of Korea," http://www.whitehouse.gov/ the_press_office/Joint-vision-for-the-alliance-of-the-United-States-of-America-and-the-Republic-of-Korea.

KOREA AND PKO: IS KOREA CONTRIBUTING TO GLOBAL PEACE?

1. Samuel Kim, ed., *East Asia and Globalization,* 2nd ed. (Lanham, MD: Rowman & Littlefield, 2000), p. 18.
2. Ibid, pp. 77–78.
3. For a detailed discussion of Kim Young-sam's *segyehwa* policy, see Balbina Y. Hwang, "Globalization," in *Globalization, Strategic Culture, and Ideas: Explaining Continuity in Korean Foreign Economic Policy* (doctoral dissertation, Georgetown University, Washington, DC, 2005).
4. South Korea's level of globalization can be measured by economic data on its levels of international trade, foreign investments, multinational corporation (MNC) activities, and cross-border flows of capital: the supposedly *segyehwa*-driven South Korean economy somehow managed to garner the lowest possible ranking in the globalization category, dropping from eleventh place (among fifteen emerging-market economies in 1993) to last place (among forty-six advanced and emerging-market economies in the world in 1998), while its global competitiveness ranking dropped from sixth in 1993 to thirty-fifth place in 1998 (Hwang, "Globalization").

5. Since 1948, more than 120 countries have taken part in 63 UN-led PKOs, and currently fifteen UN operations are deployed on four continents, with an annual budget just over $7 billion. The total number of personnel serving in UN-led PKOs as of October 2011 is 119,624. See United Nations, "Peacekeeping Operations Fact Sheet," http://www.un.org/en/peacekeeping/operations/.

6. Note that Bangladesh is the number-one contributor (more than ten thousand personnel), and Italy (seventeenth) and France (nineteenth) are the only Group of Eight (G8) countries to rank higher than the ROK. China ranks sixteenth (1,936 personnel) and Japan twenty-ninth (258 personnel). See United Nations, "Ranking of Military and Police Contributions to UN Operations, Monthly Report," October 31, 2011.

7. The law took effect on April 1, 2010. See Eun-sook Chung, "Korea's Law on UNPKO and Participation in International Peacekeeping Missions," *Korea Focus*, no. 166, February 2010.

8. Ibid.

9. ROK Ministry of National Defense (MND), *Defense White Paper*, 2010, p. 113.

10. Ibid.

11. Ibid, p. 114.

12. The clearest manifestation of the lack of technical distinction between activities that are considered PKO versus stabilization/reconstruction is their discussion in the ROK MND *Defense White Paper*, which makes no such explicit differentiation and discusses deployments of units to combat international piracy (*Cheonghae* Unit, Somalia) along with Afghanistan (*Ashean* Unit) all under the rubric of PKOs. See ROK MND, *Defense White Paper*, chap. 4, sect. 5.

13. South Korea was one of the first countries to join Operation Enduring Freedom (OEF) in Afghanistan in late 2001, deploying C-130 aircraft and a logistical support team. Concurrently, Seoul also allocated tens of millions of dollars to finance Afghan reconstruction and development. Additionally, in August 2004, the deployment of more than 3,600 ROK forces was the second-largest military presence in Iraq—second only to Great Britain—consisting of combat troops, medical teams, and engineers.

14. The commanding officer was Hwang Jin-ha, the former defense attaché to ROK Embassy in Washington, DC (1999–2002). He is currently an elected member of the ROK National Assembly (Grand National Party, GNP) and serves as chairman of the GNP's international security committee.

15. Other contributors to the UN International Force in Lebanon (UNIFIL) are Belgium, Brunei, China, Croatia, Cyprus, El Salvador, France, FYR of Macedonia, Germany, Ghana, Greece, Guatemala, Hungary, India, Indonesia, Ireland, Italy, Luxembourg, Malaysia, Nepal, New Zealand, Norway, Poland, Portugal, Qatar, Republic of Korea, Sierra Leone, Slovenia, Spain, Tanzania, and Turkey (United Nations).

16. Japan was the second-largest donor (12.5 percent) and China the seventh (3.94 percent). See United Nations, "Current Peacekeeping Operations," http://www.un.org/en/peacekeeping/documents/bakcgroundnote.pdf.

17. About forty-five nations, including those as diverse as Germany, India, Bangladesh, and Cambodia, take part in this annual exercise to practice joint PKO activities.

18. The Global Peace Operations Initiative (GPOI) is a U.S.-led global peacekeeping training program initiated during the 2004 G8 Leaders' Summit. For a more detailed discussion on GPOI and its significance for PKOs, see Balbina Hwang, "Roadmap for Expanding U.S.-ROK Alliance Cooperation on Global Issues," in *The US–South Korea Alliance: Meeting New Security Challenges*, ed. Scott Snyder (Boulder, CO: Lynne Reinner, 2012).

19. Since 1981, Cobra-Gold exercises have been held annually in Thailand. In 2010, six nations participated: the United States, Thailand, Singapore, Japan, the Republic of Korea, and Indonesia.
20. United Nations Stabilization Mission in Haiti.
21. ROK MND, *Defense White Paper*, 2010, pp. 108–9.
22. The United Nations Command led by the United States included troops from twenty other countries: Australia, Belgium, Canada, Colombia, Denmark, Ethiopia, France, Greece, India, Italy, Luxembourg, the Netherlands, New Zealand, Norway, Philippines, South Africa, Sweden, Thailand, Turkey, and the United Kingdom.
23. As of October 2011, China had 1,936 troops deployed on twelve UN PKO missions worldwide (United Nations Peacekeeping Fact Sheet, October 2011).
24. Scott J. Henderson, "Polyglot Dragon," *Armed Forces Journal*, http://www.armedforcesjournal.com/2011/11/6187393.
25. Japan has only ever been involved in six UN-led PKOs. It is currently active in Haiti (225), Syria (31), and East Timor (2) (UN Peacekeeping Fact Sheet, October 2011).
26. ROK MND, *Defense White Paper*, 2008, pp. 98–99.
27. Victor Cha, "Outperforming Expectations: The U.S.-ROK Alliance," in *Going Global: The Future of the U.S.-South Korea Alliance*, Kurt M. Campbell et al., eds. (Washington, DC: Center for a New American Security, February 2009), p. 10.
28. President Kim Young-sam launched *segyehwa* in 1993 amid much fanfare, but the crisis with North Korea over its nuclear programs at the time diverted leadership attention and the resources necessary for its implementation.
29. According to the study, the social conflict index for Korea was 0.71, considerably higher than the OECD's average of 0.44. Only three member nations—Turkey (1.2), Poland (0.76), and Slovakia (0.72)—had higher social conflict indexes than Korea. The United States ranked eighth overall and Japan tenth, ahead of European nations such as Denmark (twenty-seventh) and Sweden (twenty-sixth). See Dong-A Ilbo, "OECD Ranks Korea 4th Worst for Social Conflict," June 25, 2009.
30. Korea's homogeneity may actually work against broad public empathy toward other countries and cultures and makes building a domestic constituency in support of PKOs more difficult.
31. It is important to note here that political or social injustice was judged within the strictly formulated hierarchy established under Confucianism, and should not be equated with the Judeo-Christian notion of equality among all.
32. Such a mentality is deeply rooted in Korea's strategic culture of nationalistic survival, a paradigm presented and analyzed in my dissertation. See Hwang, *Globalization, Strategic Culture, and Ideas.*
33. James L. Schoff and Choi Hyun-jin, "Reform Locally, Act Globally? Crisis Management Trends in Korea," *Korea Economic Institute Academic Paper Series*, vol. 3, no. 3, April 2008. Schoff and Choi analyze the impact of this relatively new phenomenon in their paper.
34. The White House, Office of the Press Secretary, "Joint Vision for the Alliance of the United States of America and the Republic of Korea," http://www.whitehouse.gov/the_press_office/Joint-vision-for-the-alliance-of-the-United-States-of-America-and-the-Republic-of-Korea/.
35. Note that fears of abandonment and entrapment are not unique to the U.S.-ROK alliance. This is a well-developed concept widely applied to a variety of different types of alliances dating back to Thucydides. Most relevant here is that Japan suffers from a similar dynamic vis-à-vis its alliance with the United States, and that it also dominates domestic debate about Japan's participation in global security issues. For further

comparison of the U.S.-ROK and U.S.-Japan alliances, see Victor Cha, *Alignment Despite Antagonism: The U.S.-Korea-Japan Security Triangle* (Palo Alto, CA: Stanford University Press, 1999).

SOUTH KOREA'S COUNTERPIRACY OPERATIONS IN THE GULF OF ADEN

1. In the literature, the terms *antipiracy* and *counterpiracy* are often used interchangeably. However, there is a difference. Technically, antipiracy refers to passive defensive measures undertaken to prevent pirates from being successful. Counterpiracy refers to active measures that disrupt, confront, and seek to dismantle pirate operations and networks. CTF-151, though encompassing some of each, is more of a counterpiracy operation, and that term is used throughout this paper.
2. *Korea Times*, "Korean Navy Rescues Ship off Somalia Again," May 14, 2009, http://www.koreatimes.co.kr/www/news/nation/2009/05/113_44884.html.
3. United Nations Security Council (UNSC), "Resolution 1816," http://www.un.org/News?press/docs/2088/sc9344.doc.htm.
4. UNSC, "Resolution 1838," http://www.un.org/News/Press/docs/s008/sc9467.doc.htm. Subsequent resolutions in December 2008 extended the original six-month mandate for an additional twelve months (UNSC 1846) and authorized participating states to conduct land-based operations to address the piracy problem (UNSC 1851).
5. UNSC, "Resolution 1897," http://www.un.org/News/docs/2009/sc9799.doc.htm, and "Resolution 1950," http://www.un.org/News/Press/docs/2010/sc10092.doc.htm.
6. Douglas Guilfoyle, "Counter-Piracy Law Enforcement and Human Rights," *International and Comparative Law Quarterly*, vol. 59, 2010, p. 147.
7. Jung Sung-ki, "Anti-Piracy Unit Inaugurated," *Korea Times*, March 3, 2009, http://www.koreatimes.co.kr/www/news/nation/2010/02/116_40629.html.
8. Jung Sung-ki, "Korea to Join Anti-Piracy Campaign in Somalia," *Korea Times*, February 9, 2009, http://www.koreatimes.co.kr/www/news/nation/2011/04/205_39107.html.
9. Global Security.org, "ROK Navy," January 8, 2011, http://www.globalsecurity.org/military/world/rok/navy.htm.
10. Jin Dae-woong, "Lee backs plan for blue-water Navy," *Korea Herald*, March 19, 2008, http://www.koreaherald.co.kr/archives.
11. This ship is also identified as the *Okpo*-class.
12. *Chosun Ilbo*, "Better Ways Are Needed to Defeat Somali Pirates," January 25, 2011, http://english.chosun.com/site/data/html_dir/2011/01/25/2011012501089.html.
13. ROK MND, *Defense White Paper*, 2010, p. 111.
14. Jeong Yong-soo, "Captain recalls facing down pirates," *JoongAng Daily*, September 18, 2009, http://koreajoongangdaily.joinsmsn.com/news/article/article.aspx?aid=2910238.
15. *Korea Times*, "Korean Navy Rescues Ship off Somalia Again."
16. Jeong, "Captain recalls facing down pirates."
17. Lee Min-yong, "Pirate talks begin, Navy ship returns to its port," *JoongAng Daily*, April 12, 2010, http://koreajoongangdaily.joinsmsn.com/news/article/article.aspx?aid=2919059.
18. Abdi Sheikh and Mohamed Ahmed, "Pirates release S. Korean supertanker, Singapore ship," Reuters, November 6, 2010, http://af.reuters.com/article/topNews/idAFJOE6A504Y20101106.

19. Donald Kirk, "Seoul torn over pirates," *Asia Times Online*, February 3, 2011, http://www.atimes.com/atimes/Korea/MB03Dg01.html.
20. Combined Maritime Forces Public Affairs, "Republic of Korea Turns Over Command of CTF-151 to Turkey," September 1, 2010, http://www.cusnc.navy.mil/articles/2010/CMF052.html.
21. Christine Kim, "Navy storms hijacked ship, rescues all 21 sailors," *JoongAng Daily*, January 22, 2011, http://koreajoongangdaily.joinsmsn.com/news/article/article.aspx?aid=2931338.
22. Kirk, "Seoul torn over pirates."
23. Christine Kim, "Seoul is firm in throwing down Samho gauntlet," *JoongAng Daily*, January 22, 2011, http://koreajoongangdaily.joinsmsn.com/news/article/article.aspx?aid=2931336.
24. Lee Tae-hoon, "Navy rescues all 21 abducted sailors," *Korea Times*, January 21, 2011, http://www.koreatimes.co.kr/www/news/nation/2011/01/116_80096.html.
25. Ibid.
26. Kirk, "Seoul torn over pirates."
27. *Korea Times*, "Navy special forces to be dispatched to UAE: ministry," June 27, 2011, http://www.koreatimes.co.kr/www/news/nation/2011/06/117_89673.html.
28. Christine Kim, "Pirate who shot Capt. Seok gets life," *JoongAng Daily*, May 28, 2011, http://koreajoongangdaily.joinsmsn.com/news/article/article.aspx?aid=2936817.
29. *Korea Times*, "Somali pirates case to go to Supreme Court," September 17, 2011, http://www.koreatimes.co.kr/www/news/nation/2011/09/113_94929.html.
30. John J. Metzler, "Somali pirates are winning in 'race' with international community," Freepressers.com, January 31, 2011, http://www.freepressers.com/2011/01/somali-pirates-are-winning-in-race-with-international-community/.
31. Jung Sung-ki, "S. Korean Naval Forces Capture Pirates off Somalia," *Korea Times*, August 5, 2009, http://www.koreatimes.co.kr/www/news/nation/2009/09/205_49674.html.
32. Abdiqani Hassan, "Somali pirates threaten to kill Korean hostages," Reuters, January 23, 2011, http://af.reuters.com/article/topNews/idAFJOE70M02L20110123.
33. John M. Glionna, "South Korea may have overplayed hand against pirates, critics say," *Los Angeles Times*, January 27, 2011, http://articles.latimes.com/2011/jan/27/world/la-fg-south-korea-pirates-20110127.
34. Kirk, "Seoul torn over pirates."
35. *Korea Times*, "Korean fishing vessel meets EU warship after release," February 10, 2011, http://www.koreatimes.co.kr/www/news/nation/2011/02/113_81133.html.
36. A citadel is an area on the ship that is bulletproof and has emergency food supplies and independent communication equipment. The room protects the crew from the pirates and keeps them safe during any rescue attempt when it is difficult to separate the crew from the pirates. Vessels with decks fewer than eight meters above the water are required to install these rooms, as pirates rarely attack ships that are taller. Citadels are estimated to cost between $180,000 and $270,000 to install. See *Chosun Ilbo*, "Korean Ships to Get Pirate-Proof 'Citadel,'" January 25, 2011, http://english.chosun.com/site/data/html_dir/2011/01/25/2011012500606.html.
37. Moon Gwang-lip, "Somalian pirates scared away from Korean ship," *JoongAng Daily*, April 23, 2011, http://koreajoongangdaily.joinsmsn.com/news/article/article.aspx?aid=2935246.
38. MaritimeAsia.com, "Cheonghae anti-piracy unit saves chemical tanker from attack," July 5, 2011, http://maritimesecurity.asia/free-2/piracy-update/cheonghae-anti-piracy-unit-saves-chemical-tanker-from-pirate-attack/.

39. Christine Kim, "Korea gives $500,000 to piracy fight," *JoongAng Ilbo*, April 25, 2011, http://koreajoongangdaily.joinsmsn.com/news/article/article.aspx?aid=2935294 .
40. U.S. Department of State, "Contact Group on Piracy off the Coast of Somalia," http://www.state.gov/t/pm/ppa/piracy/contactgroup/index.htm.
41. UN Security Council, "Contact Group on Piracy off the Coast of Somalia Announces Launch of Website," October 4, 2011, http://www.un.org/News/Press/docs/2011/sc10401.doc.htm.
42. *Korea Times*, "Dealing with Piracy," February 8, 2011, http://www.koreatimes.co.kr/www/news/opinon/2011/07/202_81015.html.
43. Jonathan Berkshire Miller, "How South Korea Projects Power by Fighting Pirates," *Global Asia*, vol. 6, no. 3 (September 2011), http://www.globalasia.org/V6N3_Fall_2011/Jonathan_Berkshire_Miller.html?PHPSESSID=3b0e967ef73f246a06e026f7d8383ef3.
44. Stockholm Internatonal Peace Research Institute, "The 15 countries with the highest military expenditure in 2010," in *SIPRI Yearbook 2011* (Oxford: Oxford University Press, 2011), p. 183, http://www.sipri.org/yearbook/2011/files/SIPRIYB1104-04A-04B.pdf.
45. See Lesley Anne Warner, "Pieces of Eight: An Appraisal of U.S. Counterpiracy Options in the Horn of Africa," *Naval War College Review*, vol. 63, no. 2, Spring 2010; Yong Kwon, "Did South Korea target the right pirates?" *Asia Times Online*, February 1, 2011, http://www.atimes.com/atimes/Korea/MB01Dg01.html.

THE ROK PROVINCIAL RECONSTRUCTION TEAM IN AFGHANISTAN

1. Reuters, "South Korea paid $20 million ransom: Taliban leader," September 1, 2007, http://www.reuters.com/article/2007/09/01/us-afghan-koreans-ransom-idUSCOL31793120070901.
2. Government Accountability Office, "Provincial Reconstruction Teams in Iraq and Afghanistan," October 1, 2008, http://www.gao.gov/new.items/d0986r.pdf.
3. Ibid.
4. American Forces Press Service, "Gates to Press Asia, NATO for More Afghanistan Support," October 19, 2009, http://www.defense.gov/news/newsarticle.aspx?id=56273.
5. UK Department for International Development, "The UK Approach to Stabilisation," November 2008, http://www.stabilisationunit.gov.uk/resources/Stabilisation_guide.pdf.
6. Ibid.
7. Michael J. Finnegan, "Post-Conflict Stabilization and Reconstruction," in *The US–South Korea Alliance: Meeting New Security Challenges*, ed. Scott Snyder (Boulder, CO: Lynne Rienner, 2012), pp. 195–208.
8. Republic of Korea Ministry of National Defense, "International Peacekeeping Operations," http://www.mnd.go.kr/mndEng_2009/DefensePolicy/Policy12/Policy12_2/index.jsp.
9. Geonames, "Charikar," http://www.geonames.org/search.html?q=Charikar&country.
10. Central Statistics Organization, *Afghanistan Statistical Yearbook 2009–10* (Kabul: Government of Afghanistan, 2011), pp. 111–31, http://cso.gov.af/Content/files/Agriculture.pdf.

11. Interview with U.S. official, Parwan PRT, September 2011.
12. *New York Times,* "Attack is latest jolt to a usually quiet Afghan area," August 15, 2011, http://www.nytimes.com/2011/08/15/world/asia/15afghan.html.
13. BBC News, "Missing Germans Found in Afghanistan," September 5, 2011, http://www.bbc.co.uk/news/world-south-asia-14787092.
14. Sang-don Jung, "ROK's Overseas Deployment Policy in Afghanistan," *Korean Journal of Defense Analysis,* vol. 22, 2010, http://www.tandfonline.com/loi/rkjd20.
15. Interview with senior PRT staff, Charikar, September 20, 2011.
16. Ibid.
17. Interview with senior police official at PRT, Charikar, September 20, 2011.
18. Interview with UNAMA official, UNAMA Compound, Kabul, September 19, 2011, http://www.undp.org.af/whoweare/undpinafghanistan/Projects/sbgs/prj_nibp.htm.
19. Defense Video and Imagery Distribution System, "ROK PRT Donates 8 Ambulances to Parwan," April 7, 2011, http://www.dvidshub.net/news/68367/rok-prt-donates-8-ambulances-parwan#.Tqw2uh9sFEA.
20. Ibid.
21. Jung, "ROK's Overseas Deployment Policy in Afghanistan."
22. KOICA "KOICA-UNDP Joint Training Programme on Sustainable Agriculture Development (Afghanistan)," May 24, 2010, https://www.koica.go.kr/english/board/new/1223690_1967.html.
23. Interview with KOICA personnel at PRT, Charikar, September 22, 2011.
24. Ibid.
25. Central Statistics Organization, *Afghanistan Statistical Yearbook 2009–10,* http://cso.gov.af/Content/files/Health.pdf.
26. Ibid.
27. See http://www.youtube.com/watch?v=cdw_pVbmVGY.
28. See http://www.odakorea.go.kr/eng/operations/Asia/Afghanistan.php.
29. Interview with KOICA staff at the KMVTT, Charikar, September 22, 2011.
30. Interview with U.S. military official, Charikar, September 22, 2011.
31. The Asia Foundation Afghanistan Poll for 2011 was weeks away from publication at time of writing.
32. Interview with a serving Office of the Coordinator for Reconstruction and Stabilization (S/CRS) official by telephone, October 10, 2011.
33. Coffey International, "Helmand Monitoring and Evaluation Programme, 2010–2014," http://www.coffey.com.au/our-projects/helmand-monitoring-and-evaluation-programme.
34. "KOICA to transfer development strategy to Afghanistan," Korea.net, June 24, 2010, http://www.korea.net/NewsFocus/Policies/view?articleId=81677.
35. Interview with a senior Ministry of Rural Reconstruction and Development (MRRD) official, Kabul, September 19, 2011.
36. As of writing, Korea has agreed to build four schools with that same funding.
37. Interview with senior provincial government official by email.
38. Interview with UNAMA official, Kabul, September 19, 2011.
39. Interview with senior PRT official, Charikar, September 20, 2011.
40. Interview with senior S/CRS official at U.S. Embassy, Kabul, October 7, 2011.
41. Hillary Clinton, "America's Pacific Century," *Foreign Policy,* vol. 15, no. 6, November 2011, http://www.foreignpolicy.com/articles/2011/10/11/americas_pacific_century.

COUNTERPROLIFERATION AND SOUTH KOREA: FROM LOCAL TO GLOBAL

1. Jeffrey Lewis and Philip Maxon, "The Proliferation Security Initiative," *UNIDIR Disarmament Forum* vol. 2010, no. 2, pp. 35–44, http://www.unidir.org/pdf/articles/pdf-art2962.pdf.

2. *Yonhap News*, "South Korea Supports Proliferation Deterrent 'in Principle,'" December 6, 2006.

3. *Korea Times*, "Seoul to Observe PSI Exercise in Gulf," October 30, 2006.

4. Kim Sung-bae, "Identity Prevails in the End: North Korea's Nuclear Threat and South Korea's Response in 2006" (EAI Asia Security Initiative working paper 18, East Asia Institute, Seoul, July 2011), http://www.eai.or.kr/data/bbs/eng_report/2011072216281933.pdf.

5. Hankyoreh, "Incoming Administration May Consider Joining U.S. Missile Defense Program," January 21, 2008, http://english.hani.co.kr/arti/english_edition/e_national/264547.html.

6. *Korea Herald*, "No Immediate Plan to Join PSI: Transition Team," Month DD, YYY; *Yonhap News*, "South Korean Foreign Minister-Designate Voices Support for PSI," Month DD, YYYY.

7. Global Security Newswire, "South Korea Joins Proliferation Security Initiative," May 26, 2009, http://gsn.nti.org/gsn/nw_20090526_6455.php.

8. Global Security Newswire, "South Korea to Take Lead Role in Counterproliferation Program," October 26, 2010, http://gsn.nti.org/gsn/nw_20101026_2807.php.

9. Defense Threat Reduction Agency, Defense Treaty Inspection Readiness Program (DTIRP) Outreach Program, "Proliferation Security Initiative (PSI) Activities Since 2003," March 2011, http://dtirp.dtra.mil/pdfs/psi_activities_mar_2011.pdf.

10. Shin Hae-In, "South Korea to Become Leading PSI Member," *Korea Herald*, October 25, 2010, http://www.koreaherald.com/national/Detail.jsp?newsMLId=20101025000763.

11. Emma L. Belcher, "The Proliferation Security Initiative," Council on Foreign Relations Press, July 2011.

12. Joshua Pollack, "Ballistic Trajectory: The Evolution of North Korea's Ballistic Missile Market," *Nonproliferation Review*, vol. 18, no. 2, July 2011, http://cns.miis.edu/npr/pdfs/npr_18-2_pollack_ballistic-trajectory.pdf.

13. Mary Beth Nikitin, "Proliferation Security Initiative (PSI)," CRS Report no. RL34327 (Washington, DC: Congressional Research Service, June 15, 2012), http://www.fas.org/sgp/crs/nuke/RL34327.pdf; Robert G. Joseph, "The Global Initiative to Combat Nuclear Terrorism: A Comprehensive Approach to Today's Most Serious National Security Threat" (remarks to the Capitol Hill Club, Washington, DC, July 18, 2006), http://www.mtholyoke.edu/acad/intrel/bush/joseph.htm.

14. Nikitin, "Proliferation Security Initiative."

15. *Yonhap News*, "South Korean Office Orders Search of Suspicious North Containers," Date.

16. David E. Sanger, "U.S. Said to Turn Back North Korea Missile Shipment," *New York Times*, June 13, 2011, http://www.nytimes.com/2011/06/13/world/asia/13missile.html?_r=4&ref=global-home.

17. Nicholas Kralev, "Illegal N. Korean Arms Fly in Chinese Airspace," *Washington Times*, December 17, 2009.

18. Neil MacFarquhar, "North Korean Military Parts Were Intercepted, U.N. Says," *New York Times*, February 26, 2010.

19. *Wall Street Journal*, "Obama and the Rogues: North Korea and Iran Intrude on His Diplomatic Hopes," June 23, 2009, http://online.wsj.com/article/SB124562488560735527.html.
20. Mark Valencia, "Maritime Interdiction of North Korean WMD Trade: Who Will Do What?" Nautilus Institute Policy Forum Online 06-98A, November 3, 2006, http://www.nautilus.org/publications/essays/napsnet/forum/security/0698Valencia.html.
21. Min Gyo Koo, "Troubled Waters? Seeking a New Maritime Order in East Asia," *EAI Commentary*, no. 21 (Seoul: East Asia Institute, August 17, 2011), http://www.eai.or.kr/data/bbs/eng_report/2011081815413199.pdf.
22. MacFarquhar, "North Korean Military Parts Were Intercepted"; Nicholas Kralev, "Illegal N. Korean Arms Fly in Chinese Airspace," *Washington Times*, December 17, 2009.
23. Young-SunHa, "Path to an Advanced North Korea by 2032: Building a Complex Networked State" (EAI Asia Security working paper 10, East Asia Institute, Seoul, April 2011), http://www.eai.or.kr/data/bbs/eng_report/201104131805178.pdf.
24. Stephan Haggard and Marcus Noland, "What to Do About North Korea? Sanctions Denuclearization and Proliferation," *Witness to Transformation*, June 12, 2009, http://www.piie.com/blogs/?p=730.
25. Nikitin, "Proliferation Security Initiative."
26. Bruce E. Bechtol Jr., "Planning for the Unthinkable: Countering a North Korean Nuclear Attack and Management of Post-Attack Scenarios," *Korean Journal of Defense Analysis*, vol. 23, no. 1, March 2011, pp. 1–17.
27. Peter Hayes and Scott Bruce, "Unprecedented Nuclear Strikes of the Invincible Army: A Realistic Assessment of North Korea's Operational Nuclear Capability" (special report, Nautilus Institute for Security and Sustainability, September 22, 2011), http://www.nautilus.org/publications/essays/napsnet/reports/Hayes_Bruce_DPRK_Nuke_Capability.
28. "U.S. Focuses on Small Sea Vessels in Anti-WMD Smuggling Program," Global Security Newswire, September 22, 2011, http://gsn.nti.org/gsn/nw_20110922_3453.php.
29. *Yonhap News*, "N. Korea Conducting Infiltration Drills: Defense Minister," April 5, 2011, http://english.yonhapnews.co.kr/national/2011/04/05/70/0301000000AEN20110405009000315F.HTML.
30. Center for Nonproliferation Studies, "South Korea Hosts Export Control Workshop as U.S. Raises Concerns about ROK Export Control System," *Asian Export Control Observer*, no. 7, April/May 2005, http://cns.miis.edu/observer/pdfs/aeco_0504.pdf.
31. Choi Seung-hwan, "The Export Control System," in *Trade Law and Regulation in Korea*, Seung Wha Chang et al., eds. (Northhampon: Edward Elgar Publishing, 2011); *Asian Export Control Observer*, "South Korea Hosts Export Control Workshop," October 1, 2005, http://cns.miis.edu/observer/pdfs/ieco_0510e.pdf.
32. Cameron Hunter and Sammy Salama, "Companies Reported to Have Sold or Attempted to Sell Libya Gas Centrifuge Components," Nuclear Threat Initiative, March 1, 2005, http://www.nti.org/e_research/e3_60a.html.
33. Jun Bong-geun, "The Involvement of the Business in Export Controls in the Republic of Korea" (presentation to the fifth ROK-UN Joint Conference on Disarmament and Nonproliferation Issues, December 13–15, 2006).
34. BBC News, "Toxic Chemical 'Sold to N Korea,'" September 24, 2004, http://news.bbc.co.uk/2/hi/asia-pacific/3685392.stm.
35. Jungmin Kang, "Current Status of the South Korean Export Control Systems," *Nautilus Institute*, November 3, 2006.

36. Center for Nonproliferation Studies, "South Korea Launches Online Database for Strategic Items Exports," *Asian Export Control Observer,* no. 6, February/March 2005, http://cns.miis.edu/observer/pdfs/aeco_0502.pdf.

37. Center for Nonproliferation Studies, "South Korean Company Allegedly Assisted Iran in 2004 and 2005 in Acquiring Nuclear Material," *International Export Control Observer,* October 2005, http://cns.miis.edu/observer/pdfs/ieco_0510e.pdf.

38. Ibid.

39. Dave H. Kim, "South Korean Export Control Awareness on Rise but Compliance Lacking," *International Export Control Observer,* November 2005, http://cns.miis.edu/observer/pdfs/old/ieco_0511e_old2.pdf.

40. Ibid.

41. Ibid.

42. Kang, "Current Status of the South Korean Export Control Systems."

43. Center for Nonproliferation Studies, "South Korea Hosts Export Control Workshop as U.S. Raises Concerns about ROK Export Control System," *Asian Export Control Observer,* no. 7, April/May 2005, http://cns.miis.edu/observer/pdfs/aeco_0504.pdf; Juho Song, "Industry Compliance and Government Efforts" (Seoul: Republic of Korea, Ministry of Commerce, Industry and Energy, July 19, 2006), http://www.exportcontrol.org/library/conferences/1379/06_12.pdf.

44. Ibid.

45. BBC News, "Toxic Chemical 'Sold to N Korea,'" September 24, 2004, http://news.bbc.co.uk/2/hi/asia-pacific/3685392.stm.

46. Ibid.

47. *Chosun Ilbo,* "Korean Held for Export of Strategic Nuclear Goods," October 13, 2006.

48. Tyler Chapman, "Business as Usual," Radio Free Asia, February 9, 2010, http://www.rfa.org/english/blog/burma_diary/corruption-02092010155353.html.

49. Togzhan Kassanova, "Nonproliferation Challenges in East Asia: Development of Strategic Trade Controls (STC)" (presentation delivered at the PONI Spring Conference, April 8, 2010), http://csis.org/images/stories/poni/100408_Kassenova_Spring.pdf.

50. North Korea Economy Watch, "Japan Arrests North Korean on Charges of Illegal Export," October 5, 2011, http://www.nkeconwatch.com/2011/10/05/japan-arrests-n-korean-on-charges-of-illegal-export/.

51. Choi, "The Export Control System."

52. Ibid.

53. Council for Security Cooperation in the Asia Pacific Export Controls Experts Group, "First CSCAP Export Controls Experts Working Group Meeting," Tokyo, November 7–8, 2005, http://www.cscap.org/uploads/docs/XCXGReports/1XCXGRpt.pdf.

54. Chen Kane, Stephanie C. Lieggi, and Miles A. Pomper, "Time for Leadership: South Korea and Nuclear Nonproliferation," *Arms Control Association,* March 2011, http://www.armscontrol.org/act/2011_03/SouthKorea.

55. Arms Control Association, "South Korea Joins MTCR," April 2001, http://www.armscontrol.org/node/2923.

56. Global Security, "South Korean Long Range Missiles," July 24, 2011, http://www.globalsecurity.org/wmd/world/rok/missiles.htm.

57. WMD Insights, "UN Security Council Resolution 1540: PART I: Resolution 1810: Progress since 1540," August 2008, http://www.nuclearfiles.org/menu/key-issues/nuclear-weapons/issues/governance/international-coop/res-1540.htm.

58. Tanya Ogilvie-White, "Facilitating implementation of Resolution 1540 in South-East Asia and the South Pacific," in *Implementing Resolution 1540: The Role of Regional Organizations,* ed. Lawrence Scheinman (New York: United Nations Institute for

Disarmament Research, 2008). See http://www.unidir.org/pdf/ouvrages/pdf-1-978-92-9045-190-7-en.pdf.

59. Ibid.

60. Ibid.

61. Ibid.

62. Xinhua News, "S. Korea to Join Regional Non-Proliferation Meeting This Week," June 29, 2009.

63. World Nuclear Association, "Nuclear Power in South Korea," August 2012, http://world-nuclear.org/info/inf81.html.

64. Ibid.

65. Ibid; Park Jenmin, "An Introduction of Energy Situation and Policy of ROK" (presentation delivered at the 2010 East Asia Science and Security Workshop, September 23–24, 2010), http://www.nautilus.org/projects/science-security/2010-east-asia-science-and-security-meeting-1/02.1%20ROK.ppt.

66. Global Initiative to Combat Nuclear Terrorism, "GCINT Statement of Principles," May 13, 2010, http://www.thenuclearsecuritysummit.org/eng_common/images/fla/25._GICNT_SOP.pdf.

67. *Korea Herald*, "S. Korea Calls for Firm, United Global Response to N.K. Nukes," June 30, 2011, http://www.koreaherald.com/national/Detail.jsp?newsMLId=20110630000593.

68. Ibid.

69. Sergio Duarte, "Eighth United Nations-Republic of Korea Joint Conference on Disarmament and Non-Proliferation Issues," November 16, 2009, http://www.un.org/disarmament/HomePage/HR/docs/2009/2009Nov16ROK.pdf.

70. Cho Hyun, "Closing remarks: Cho Hyun, Deputy Minister for Multilateral, Global and Legal Affairs, Republic of Korea" (speech delivered at the ninth ROK-UN Joint Conference on Disarmament and Non-proliferation Issues, December 2–3, 2010), http://www.unrcpd.org.np/uploads/conferences/file/Hyun%20Cho-Closing%20Remarks.pdf.

71. Cho Hyun, "Welcoming remarks: Cho Hyun, Deputy Minister for Multilateral, Global and Legal Affairs, Republic of Korea" (speech delivered at the ninth ROK-UN Joint Conference on Disarmament and Non-proliferation Issues, December 2–3, 2010), http://www.unrcpd.org.np/uploads/conferences/file/Hyun%20Cho-Welcoming%20Remarks.pdf.

72. *Nucleonics Week*, "South Korea Wants to Export 80 Reactors by 2030," June 16, 2011.

73. Arirang, "Korea Becomes World's Leading Nuclear Power Plant Exporter," November 10, 2010, http://www.arirang.co.kr/News/News_View.asp?nseq=108941&code=Ne2&category=2.

74. World Nuclear Association (WNA), "Nuclear Power in South Korea," August 2012, http://www.world-nuclear.org/info/inf81.html; *UPI Energy*, "South Korea-Jordan Sign $130M Nuclear Deal," March 31, 2010.

75. ArabianBusiness.com, "Korea Has 'Great Interest' in Saudi Nuclear Deals Bid," January 18, 2011; *Asia Pulse*, "S. Korea, Egypt Seek Cooperation in Nuke Power, Oil" January 20, 2011.

76. *Yonhap*, "S. Korea, India Sign Nuclear Power Cooperation Pact" July 26, 2011.

77. *JoongAng Ilbo*, "MOU Reveals Korea's Quest for Argentina Nuclear Deal," September 17, 2010, http://joongangdaily.joins.com/article/view.asp?aid=2926151; *Asia Pulse*, "S. Korea to Strengthen Nuclear Co-Op with S.Africa," July 6, 2011.

78. *Thai Press Reports*, "Thailand Executive of Korea Electricity Power Corporation Comments on Thailand's Nuclear Powerplant," August 30, 2011; *Yonhap News*, "Lee, Malaysian King Discuss Atomic Energy Cooperation," July 21, 2011.

79. Richard Tanter and Arabella Imhoff, "The Muria Peninsula Nuclear Power Proposal: State of Play," Austral Policy Forum 09-1A(January 19, 2009), http://www.nautilus.org/publications/essays/apsnet/policy-forum/2009/muria-nuclear-power/.

80. *Financial Times*, "Seoul's Nuclear Ambitions Wane," April 26, 2011, http://www.ft.com/intl/cms/s/0/0d0122de-7030-11e0-bea7-00144feabdc0.html#axzz1XmJbqfPd.

81. Ayesha Daya, "South Korea Plans to Lend $10 Billion for U.A.E. Nuclear Plants," *Bloomberg News*, October 8, 2010; "Seoul's Nuclear Ambitions Wane."

82. U.S. Department of Energy, "Fact Sheet: NNSA [National Nuclear Security Administration] Next Generation Safeguards Initiative," January 2, 2009, http://nnsa.energy.gov/mediaroom/factsheets/nextgenerationsafeguards.

83. Choe Kwan-kyoo, "The ROK's Contribution to Global Nuclear Nonproliferation."

84. *Yonhap News*, "KEPCO Team Picked as Non-Proliferation Compliance Program Partner," August 6, 2010; *Denki Shimbun*, "South Korea to Strengthen Development of Overseas Nuclear Human Resources," http://www.shimbun.denki.or.jp/en/news/20101001_03.html.

85. *Asia Pulse*, "S. Korean Nuclear Foundation Signs MOU with IAEA," July 28, 2010.

86. *Chosun Ilbo*, "Lee Speaks Out for Nuclear Energy at UN," September 23, 2011, http://english.chosun.com/site/data/html_dir/2011/09/23/2011092301114.html; Sungook Hong, "Where Is the Nuclear Nation Going? Hopes and Fears over Nuclear Energy in South Korea after the Fukushima Disaster," *East Asia Science, Technology, and Society*, vol. 5, no. 3, September 2011, pp. 409–15.

87. *Agence France Presse*, "Japan Vows to Continue Nuclear Plant Exports," August 5, 2011.

88. Peter Hayes and Moon Chung-in, "Park Chung Hee, the CIA, and the Bomb" (special report, Nautilus Institute for Security and Sustainability, September 23, 2011), http://www.nautilus.org/publications/essays/napsnet/reports/Hayes_Moon_ParkChungHee_Bomb.

89. Chen Kane, Stephanie C. Lieggi, and Miles A. Pomper, "Going Global: Issues Facing South Korea as an Emerging Nuclear Exporter," *Tomorrow's North-East Asia*, Korea Economic Institute, Ocotber 2010, http://www.keia.org/publication/going-global-issues-facing-south-korea-emerging-nuclear-exporter

90. Mark Hibbs, "Nuclear Suppliers Group and the IAEA Additional Protocol" (nuclear energy brief, Carnegie Endowment for International Peace, August 18, 2010), http://carnegieendowment.org/publications/index.cfm?fa=view&id=41393.

91. Chen Kane, Stephanie C. Lieggi, and Miles A. Pomper, "Time for Leadership: South Korea and Nuclear Nonproliferation," *Arms Control Today*, March 2011, http://www.armscontrol.org/act/2011_03/SouthKorea.

About the Authors

Scott Bruce is a project manager for the Partnership for Nuclear Security at CRDF Global. Before joining CRDF, he was a fellow at the East-West Center in Hawaii, where he analyzed the impact of cell phones and information technology in North Korea. Prior to that, he was the director of U.S. operations for the Nautilus Institute in San Francisco, where he managed projects on nonproliferation and energy security. His work at Nautilus included projects on the North Korean energy sector and nuclear program, spent-fuel storage and disposal, regional energy cooperation in East Asia, and state-level compliance with United Nations Security Council resolutions (UNSCR) 1540 and 1373. Bruce studied history at the University of California and Queen's University Belfast. He received MA degrees in international business and Asia-Pacific studies from the University of San Francisco.

John Hemmings is a doctoral candidate in the international relations department at the London School of Economics and a nonresident Sasakawa Peace Foundation (SPF) fellow at the Pacific Forum CSIS. In 2012, Hemmings was a resident Worldwide Support for Development (WSD)–Handa fellow at the Pacific Forum, where he worked on Asia-Pacific security issues. In particular, he focused on U.S.-Japanese trilateral relationships and North Korean security issues. Prior to this fellowship, Hemmings spent four years at the Royal United Services Institute in London, where he conducted research on Northeast Asia and Afghanistan. In 2011, he went to Parwan Province, Afghanistan to study South Korea's provincial reconstruction team. Hemmings received his MA in security studies from King's College London. He has lived and worked throughout Asia and the Middle East and speaks both Japanese and French. Hemmings has contributed political analysis to a number of media outlets, including the BBC, CNN, al-Jazeera, Channel 4, *Asia Times* online, East Asia Forum, and the *Diplomat*.

Balbina Hwang is visiting professor at Georgetown University, where she teaches courses on East Asian political economy. She is also currently an adjunct research fellow at the Institute for National Security Strategy in Seoul, Korea. From 2007 to 2009, she served as senior special adviser to Ambassador Christopher Hill, assistant secretary for East Asian and Pacific affairs at the U.S. State Department. From 2009 to 2010, she taught Northeast Asian security at National Defense University. Prior to joining the State Department, she was senior policy analyst for Northeast Asia in the Asian Studies Center of the Heritage Foundation. Hwang is the author of numerous articles and book chapters and has received several writing awards. She has provided expert testimony before congressional hearings and is a frequent commentator for major international media outlets. From 1998 to 1999, Hwang was a Fulbright scholar to South Korea, where she conducted doctoral dissertation field research. Hwang earned her BA from Smith College, her MIA from Columbia University, her MBA from the Darden School of Business at the University of Virginia, and her PhD from Georgetown University.

Terence Roehrig is professor of national security affairs and the director of the Asia-Pacific studies group at the U.S. Naval War College. He is also a research fellow at the Harvard Kennedy School in the international security program and the project on managing the atom. He is the author of two forthcoming books, *Japan, South Korea, and the U.S. Nuclear Umbrella: Extended Deterrence and Nuclear Weapons in the Post-Cold War World* and *South Korea's Rise in World Affairs: Power, Economic Development, and Foreign Policy*, coauthored with Uk Heo. Roehrig has published articles and book chapters on Korean and East Asian security issues, the northern limit line, the South Korean navy, North Korea's nuclear weapons program, the U.S.-South Korea alliance, human rights, and transitional justice. He received his PhD in political science from the University of Wisconsin–Madison and is a past president of the Association of Korean Political Studies.

Scott A. Snyder is senior fellow for Korea studies and director of the program on U.S.-Korea policy at the Council on Foreign Relations (CFR), where he had served as an adjunct fellow from 2008 to 2011. Prior to joining CFR, Snyder was a senior associate in the international relations program of the Asia Foundation, where he founded and directed the Center for U.S.-Korea Policy and served as the foundation's representative in Korea from 2000 to 2004. He was also a senior associate at the Pacific Forum CSIS. Snyder is the editor of *The US–South Korea Alliance: Meeting New Security Challenges* and author of *China's Rise and the Two Koreas: Politics, Economics, Security; Paved With Good Intentions: The NGO Experience in North Korea* (coeditor); and *Negotiating on the Edge: North Korean Negotiating Behavior*. Snyder received his MA from the regional studies East Asia program at Harvard University and was a Thomas G. Watson fellow at Yonsei University in South Korea.

www.ingramcontent.com/pod-product-compliance
Lightning Source LLC
Chambersburg PA
CBHW060513280326
41933CB00014B/2945